Earning a Ribbon

I0621211

Marissa Elis Pope

Dedication

This book is dedicated to my mother. I know there was a lot we didn't get to speak about, and we had very little time spent together, but the time I did spend with you, me, and you were always having fun and were happy. I still haven't forgotten the sound of your voice.

To my mother: I love you.

"You were the friend everyone wanted, and you knew what it was like to hide the pain and keep those around you happy. No one understood what you have been through, but we all loved you. Words cannot describe the pain we all feel because this nightmare has become all too real. My dearest mother, flesh and blood, your memory will be carried on by thousands of people. You were stolen from us, so we are rising to show people you didn't deserve this. We love you; I love you. Watch over us as we continue through life and guide our family through the struggles to come."

- Marissa Pope (2012)

Preface

Hello,

I'm sure you are wondering why I would write about such a dark and dramatic thing in my life. Well, it all started with me sitting on the couch watching a movie about family issues. In this movie, it's the typical mother-daughter fight and daughter-father siding together until the daughter betrays the mother and the father. Then she is all alone in her situation, afraid to tell her parents when something happens to her. Then she finally opens up to her mother about being assaulted by a boy her age.

As I was watching that play out, I started thinking about my mother and how I'd never be able to call her or speak to her ever again in my life. I began to think long and hard about my life and spaced out for a few minutes before my husband brought me back by calling my name and asking if I was okay. I replied yes and got up to my office table and turned on my laptop, the tv monitor I use to do my work, then my wireless mouse and keyboard. I began typing and writing side notes on a piece of paper to give me reminders of certain things in my mind. He asked what I was doing, and I replied:

"I've decided I won't stay quiet anymore. There are things that have happened to me that I feel like others could either learn from or use to help themselves. There are women out there who are afraid to speak up because of fear or not having someone to support them. I may not be the best example, but I am willing to put myself out there to help someone who may need some kind of light at the end of the tunnel."

So that's how I got here, writing the first story of a part of my life. I have so much more to share, but I thought this was more important. I hope you enjoy it.

TABLE OF CONTENTS

About the Author

My name is Marissa Pope, and I am from a small town in Texas. I lived there for most of my childhood and had many happy and sad life experiences. I moved away when I was 21 and made my way all the way over to Georgia. I've had so many life experiences along the way, along with your typical struggles, but the journey has been an interesting one.

I suffer from severe anxiety, depression, and C-PTSD. The walls inside my mind had been a prison for a very long time until I got the medical help I needed to level me out. I could only see the world as black and white and wouldn't allow any room for what I believed were "lies." Now that I have the proper medical care and medications, I can live a somewhat normal life without so many lows. I also have therapy with an amazing therapist, where I am held accountable for my actions and behaviors. She has helped me do this as part of my healing process and getting my trauma out there so that others who may be experiencing the same in silence may finally have the courage to speak up on their own.

Lastly, I am a calm and compassionate person. I've

come a long way, and I am continuing to heal. I don't know how, when, or how soon I will be fully healed, but it starts with just a few nudges in the right direction so you can get on the right track. I have been doing a lot more self-love in my life recently, and I feel like we all need to remember who needs to love you the most, YOU.

Hotline Services

- The National Domestic Violence Hotline: 800-799-7233
  Hours: 24/7
  Languages: English, Spanish and 200 + through interpretation service.
  https://www.thehotline.org/

- National Sexual Assault Hotline: 1-800-656-4673
  Hours: Available 24 hours
  https://www.rainn.org/about-national-sexual-assault-telephone-hotline

- 988 Suicide and Crisis Lifeline: 988
  Hours: Available 24 hours.
  Languages: English, Spanish
  https://988lifeline.org/

- SAMHSA's National Helpline: 1-800-662-4357
  SAMHSA's National Helpline is a free, confidential, 24/7, 365-day-a-year treatment referral and information service (in English and Spanish) for individuals and families facing mental and/or substance use disorders.
  https://www.samhsa.gov/find-help/national-helpline

Page Blank Intentionally

Chapter 1: Walk with Me

"My story and journey is something I never thought I would discuss, but here I am. I invite you to take a walk with me and begin the retracing of my past, who knows you might have been through something similar"

I close my eyes as I transport myself and sneak a glimpse into the past. It's a little overwhelming, but I need to remember it. As it makes me who I am today. It's not all bad, but not all good either.

Sighing, I open my eyes and stare at the blue sky with clouds covering most of everything I could have seen. I can feel the warm and dry wind, rushing past and around me, and can feel the telltale feeling of sunburn beginning to form on my face and nose.

The smell is all too familiar, and I inhale as deeply as I can, yet again. It feels nice, just lying down on the roof of my childhood home, in a small town in Texas.

"I wonder if someone else is staring at the same clouds as me. Are they thinking the same thing? Would we get along? I'm so alone," I think to myself as I listen to my

Lordi: The Arockalypse CD.

During those days, the music I listened to matched my mood. Emotionally, there was a lot going on, and music seemed like a kind of escape—refreshing me a little.

I often climbed on the roof to run away and '*disappear*' from my female guardian, Viky. In a way, this roof was my escape hole too.

A lot of times, I had to pretend to be someone I wasn't just to live peacefully with my female guardian. I had to create another personality, just to survive. This is something that didn't just didn't happen out of the blue, it strengthened after years and years of doing it. I had developed a persona for my female guardian when I was around her and it consisted of me being silent, and also being unseen. That was the only way to get her to be somewhat "normal".

My female guardian never let up on me. The reason I call her my female guardian rather than anything that would create a familial bond is because I was not treated like family. So again, she was my female guardian, not my family. As family is not someone who takes care *of* you, but someone who cares *about* you.

So, the roof was my safe spot, there were no doors to

11

be locked behind and I knew she could not climb up to where I was. Veronika—Viky, a.k.a. my female guardian, was quite an elderly woman, and that worked to my advantage as I could be in peace without being disturbed, on the roof. A place where I could live and dwell in my thoughts, as I gazed at the traffic passing by. It really became a hobby more than an activity. Often times I'd wave to my neighbors across the street and to their friend also. Eventually, people would look up on the roof of my childhood home to see if I was up there hanging out like always.

There was not much to do in the small town. But it sure was comforting to know that nothing that was in town was too far away from where I resided. We had a small strip mall that had a small retail store and a clothing store, where everyone went to when it came time for prom, homecoming, and that special occasion and with one grocery store and one supercenter that was owned privately by a rich family. As a child, I loved to go to the superstore to walk around and hang out. There used to be a fast-food chain inside of the restaurant and to this day I love to go to that certain fast-food chain.

To put it in kind terms, the place where I lived at was not the best. There were occasional gunshots, fights and whatnot. Oftentimes, illegal immigrants would make their way through the yard or knock on the front door in the middle of the night, asking for something to eat and drink. My paternal grandfather oftentimes either turned them away or gave them some sort of water from the water hose, he wouldn't dare let them anywhere in the house, which I was very thankful for him being a very kind-hearted but respectable man.

Most of the time, we didn't answer the door because you just can't trust anyone to not try to harm you when they are in a dire state. And also, because the time was not great times as the crime rates were on the rise and also human trafficking.

Often, at night, I could hear voices—the violent shouting in the distance from that couple up the street, or people running from the cops trying to find ways into homes for shelter and to escape. When I heard them, I usually turned everything off in the room, played a CD, and put on my headphones, with full volume blasting in my ears. The sounds outside my window scared me into silence but music always brought me comfort in a way that was almost second nature to me which made these kinds of situations okay.

I wanted to drown out the fear and anxiety I felt because of the violent environment around me. They say that the environment around you turns you into who you are, and this, no doubt, was certainly true about the environment I was living in. I had learned how to manipulate people without them realizing I was actually doing it, and I also had developed a way to speak to people in a condescending way that sounded like I was just saying something funny so that there wouldn't be any back-lash for the things I'd say/do.

I lived on the east side of town—it wasn't the worst part. But I wanted to live close to a great-aunt, on the west side of town. The houses over there were nicer and the neighborhood was more inviting. I had a second great-aunt who also did well in life with her husband and son. In retrospect, I think it was more of a need to live with one of them. I knew that had to see how their sister was treating her only grandchild because she hated my mother so much. They often let me explore when I was in their homes and kept Viky away from me so that I could get some relief from her.

I feel like it wasn't because of the nice living conditions there, but more of my yearning to be a part of a family life like those of my great-aunts. They were so cool, calm, and collected. I wanted that peace in my life. I wanted that comfort. That feeling that the environment I was in right now hadn't sealed my fate. That I was going have a good life, even if I had to build it for myself from the scratch.

I had never seen Viky, my guardian, act like her sisters. Like every neighborhood, the east side too had its good and bad moments, partly good because it was *'the hood'* back in the late '90s. I was still young and alive during those years. I had a whole life to live. A life to experience the good and the bad. I was the optimistic type, who saw the glass as half-full, rather than half-empty.

For now, life hadn't handed me the cards I was going to need to navigate the struggles ahead of me as I progressed through this journey. We were poor, but not actually poor, if that makes any sense at all. I had everything I needed and more, but we still struggled to eat most of the time. There were times I had to actually seek something to eat, or over eat at school, to ease my hunger.

When we would go to the supermarket Viky would always remind me, *"When we go inside, you **will not** ask for anything."* She would stress on the 'will not,' widening her eyes.

"If you start crying, then I will actually give you something to cry about. Don't forget about the belt at home either." She'd say, rather smugly, might I add.

This might sound disturbing and cruel, which it definitely was, but for me, it was just another day of the week. I was so used to it that I never realized how wrong this was to say to someone. How emotionally disturbing it was, and how it could destroy a person if they got used to these types of violent sentences. Not to mention, again, I was so used to it, this actually felt normal.

Anyway, once inside the store, we would start the act. Viky would start smiling the biggest smile as she greeted everyone in the store, and would be with her, trying to be as quite as possible, fearing the punishment I would have to endure if I disobeyed her.

"Aye, dios Mio!"

"Como se porta bien!"

"Oh, my God! It behaves so well!"

These were the comments passed about me, which was quite common and no one thought anything wrong with them. With their small minds, they competed with each other to see whose child was more well-behaved. But we all knew each other enough, as young people, that it was all smoke in the mirror. All was an act, and everything was fake, just a show. As I mentioned before, everyone tried to hide who they really were—their real self.

There is this great saying by a nihilist, **"You are**

born alone and you die alone. That is the way of life, and it's better you get used to it as soon as possible."

I know the words are not encouraging, but they give an insight into how, in life, oftentimes, you will feel all alone and miserable. And let me tell you, loneliness is not a nice companion to have. Loneliness is not something anyone can ever long for.

Then, to top it all off, like the cherry on the cake, the people around you can be cruel and unforgiving. It was common practice, amongst my peers and me, that we would hide who we were, not be it from friends, family, and even religious figures (that strong catholic community in that town).

I almost never acted the same around anyone, and no one seemed to like anything about me. At that age, and with a guardian like mine, it felt like an obligation to make people like me. Otherwise, it was like I had failed to accomplish one more thing—such a simple task. A lot of my childhood peers saw me as "intense" and "overwhelming" but what they didn't understand was the fact that at home I was experiencing that from Viky.

I often questioned myself, *'Why am I the way that I am? What is wrong with me? Why don't I hate being so fake* *around everyone? Why are we complying with this way of life? Are am truly okay with being silent **all the time**?'*

But to be honest, I never really could answer myself. It was like this was the way of life, and like it or not, this was how I had to live, how I had to spend the rest of my life.

When you stay quiet and do not express yourself, you feel like everyone hates you. You doubt yourself; your confidence is nonexistent, and you start to devalue yourself. Every time it felt like I was stabbing myself in the chest with the dull end of a pipe. It was a painful thing to endure.

I was quiet for reasons people would never understand or listen to. But everyone assumed that because I was quiet, and never had anything to say, there was nothing that was bothering me. That I was *content*—I was also *happy*.

No one had a clue that I only smiled out of fear of a threat, or because I was told to, or I had to face a punishment when I got home for just not smiling in public, or saying the wrong thing when I should have kept my mouth shut. No one had any idea, or maybe they did, but no one cared enough to heed it. Things like that happened everywhere we went; even at the church.

Viky never showed me any compassion, but she

claimed to love me and would abuse me out of love. How fucked up does that sound? And yes, everything really was as fucked up as it sounds. Back then, I didn't know this is what most abusers by nature say. That you let yourself be abused because they say that they love you and you believe it. That they starve you so much for love, that an ounce of their affection is worth your whole world, your whole future, your whole life.

Whether she believed what she was saying or was she lying, I don't know. Was it her idea, her way of loving— I guess I'll never find out. And that's the thing. I don't even want to. Because not any of those answers will give me any comfort. Viky, for all intentions and purposes, misconstrued my processes of feeling to a great extent. It even came to a point where I was unable to distinguish between love and abuse. But that's a whole different story for another time.

Now, you must be thinking, where was my biological family in all this? Let's now first get to that.

My father, Able, was never really around, unless Viky called him to come by the house so she could get some rest from me. He would come by, and the first thing he would do would be that he would snatch the television remote from me. The television was actually kind of a blessing for Viky, so she kept it. It kept me from bothering Viky because I was quiet and in one place.

"I can't watch television at my house so I'm going to watch it here and you are going to like it." He would order.

So, I would sit there silently, and watch his dumb shows about *remastering* old vintage cars, spring break reality shows, and *lots* of action/drama shows. I would watch those stupid shows with Able in silence until he got bored and then would leave.

I'd watch him drive away, longing to feel the love of my father, the same love he had for others. Even then, I felt that emptiness, the emptiness for love, of any kind, from anyone! Yeah, that *is* fucked up, but that's just how I was being brought up. I never experienced that feeling of love and compassion from Able—my father, but just for show.

Able had me when he was in his early twenties. So naturally, I was always seen as a burden. All my life, he just came and disappeared—he was never *really* there, never really a father. Parental love is characterized by warmth, affection, care, comfort, concern, nurture, support, and acceptance.

Parents' love can be felt when they kiss, hug, praise, compliment, or say nice things to or about their children.

20

Children need parents, or even caregivers to provide a specific type of positive response to grow not only physically, but mentally as well. This form of response is often interpreted as an act of parental love.

Without parental love, children feel rejected. And parental rejection is recognized as cold, unaffectionate, hostile, aggressive, indifferent, neglected or lack of care. Rejection is manifested in behavior such as hitting, pinching, mocking, shouting, cursing, belittling, uncaring, unconcerned, or saying unkind or sarcastic things to the child. Some parents may also appear bitter, resentful, irritable, impatient, or antagonistic toward their children. And I experienced that!

Honestly, even to this day, my heart aches. For that little girl who never got to experience the love that she deserved. That almost every child has. The love that's taken for granted by many. Able used to tell women that I was his little sister, or I wasn't his. So, yeah, my own father was embarrassed to own me in front of the world.

"I'm just kidding. Why do you take everything so seriously? That's why I don't take you anywhere!" He would say to me.

I don't think he ever realized how bad that hurt me

emotionally. To hear *my biological father,* tell people that I wasn't his daughter, that I was his little sister. It was just as bad as getting your teeth ripped out with plyers all at once.

I literally had no one to confide in, not even my own father. I realized that very early in my life and slowly started building a wall around my heart, hiding how I felt and who I really was all together. If I told my father anything, he would reveal everything I said to Viky, and then I would get confronted by her in a very hostile manner.

But I did have one saving grace—my grandfather. *Guadalupe*, or *Lupe* for short. He is the best man I had ever known in my life and raised me with a military focus and mindset. He is a Vietnam Veteran and I love and appreciate how he helped mold my character. If it wasn't for him, I think the environment I grew up in would have shaped me into a totally different person than I am today. He taught me many things and showed me how to live off of the land. We did so many activities together and I often went with him to the ranch he worked at; he was a hunting guide. He also showed me the importance of being true to yourself no matter what others said or thought of you.

Able did many things which made *me* embarrassed to call him my father. And to say that he would own me as his, hah! When I worked at the local Detention Center in my hometown, on my very first day, I learned something about my father.

"Isn't your dad, M&M?" The Sargent on duty there asked me.

I looked up at him in confusion, *"Who? I think you have me confused for someone else."*

"No! I'm sure you're his kid." He insisted.

Then the Sargent proceeded to show me a mug shot of him. My heart sank, and I put my face in my hands, red with embarrassment.

"Yes, that's him. Why do you call him M&M?" I finally mustered enough courage and asked.

"Because he's a mamón (cocksucker)! And a mentiroso (liar)!" The Sargent roared in my face.

The whole room busted out laughing. And even though, at that moment, I wanted the ground to open and swallow me whole, all I did was smirk and act like it didn't bother me.

But this incident was just the start. Things like that followed me around most of my life. Some of my peers called my father *'the Mexican Fat-Joe'*, some *'Rollie-*

Pollie', and some *'Fat Bastard."* So, naturally, even my childhood was not the most enjoyable and carefree time for me.

Able had a way of making things up and being very overbearing with his need to be validated and heard. A lot of times, he lied just to get people to like him or just even listen to what he had to say. It was only him and his feelings. No one else's existence or point of view mattered. I pitied him. All the way to the end.

Now, I am who I am because of the way I was treated, and the way people around me made me feel. People don't realize how important childhood is. Many take a worth-having childhood for granted and target people like me, telling us to just *"get over it"* or that I'm the one who is making it harder on myself. But how does one get over such a huge phase of their life? The phase that built them to be whom they become. How does one get over something so significant?

But well, somehow, I survived. Even though the challenges I faced would break many people, and crush them, I faced them all head-on.

But that too, I will discuss more in the coming chapters.

In a nutshell, as the African proverb says, **"The child who is not embraced by the village will burn it down to feel its warmth."**

Chapter 2: The Others

"The others is a more expansive look into the people I know, and how their actions shaped me into the person I am today"

The others is the chapter you will meet many of the people that had an impact, more than most people can imagine. It is going to be weird, sad, and funny but more importantly a glance into what my relationships were like.

Before I go towards that, I would like to discuss how important family is, so that you as a reader may have a better idea of why my life turned out the way it did.

As a child grows up, they learn how to interact with the world around them by observing the behaviors of their parents and siblings. These early relationships serve as a blueprint for future connections, shaping the way that the child perceives themselves and others. For example, a child who grows up in a household with healthy communication and boundaries is more likely to seek out relationships with similar qualities as they enter adulthood. Conversely, a child who experiences toxic or abusive relationships within their family may struggle to establish healthy connections later in life.

While it's not always a conscious decision, people often choose partners and friends who remind them of their family members, whether it's due to a shared sense of humor, similar personality traits, or even physical appearance. This can be both positive and negative, as family dynamics can repeat themselves in future relationships, reinforcing beliefs about connections and self.

As individuals move through life, it's important to recognize the influence that early family connections have on their interpersonal relationships. By acknowledging patterns and working to break unhealthy cycles, people can create healthier connections and foster positive self-growth. When life gets hard, people need support. This can be emotional and/ or fiscal support. Someone going through rough times will turn to their family if they trust them to give them love. Feeling accepted and understood during a particular extremity is basic need for people. Families – whether traditional or chosen – can give that.

In good or bad times, families can give the affection and happiness a person needs to be content. It can be delicate to find friends or purpose in adulthood. However, they'll always be suitable to find the love and support they need, If a person has a strong family. With their family behind them, a person will find the provocation and courage for success. On the other side, if a person isn't getting love and support from a family structure, they'll feel lonely, depressed, and indeed hopeless.

Families are capitals of tradition; numerous families carry on traditions through the times by participating in stories from their history. This creates connections with family members that aren't around presently. A person who grows up in this type of family feels like they belong to a commodity bigger than themselves. They'll pride in being a member of a community that's gone through rigors and triumphs.

Exploration supports that people from close-knitt families go on to enjoy close connections latterly in life. Psychological Science published a long-running study in 2016 that looked at men's connections. Experimenters learned that men who grew up in nurturing families developed stronger connections than men who didn't have accepting families. They managed their feelings well and maintained a near connection with their mates.

Now it was not ALWAYS horrible. I did have a

SOME-WHAT supportive aunt, Valeria, and uncle, Jose, on my paternal side. My paternal uncle was the best. It was hard for me to trust someone as you can imagine most abuse victims do but how else can a person survive without connection and love? There is a quote near my heart it says *"We need people in our lives with whom we can be as open as possible. To have real conversations with people may seem like such a simple, obvious suggestion, but it involves courage and risk".*

Jose was someone I wish was my actual father though he saw the good in people most times and often defended Viky, but that was his mother and he always used to say to me,

"Mom has her moments. That's just how she is. She buys you everything you want – isn't that enough to make you happy?"

But. It. Never. Was. Enough.

My Uncle Jose had always been a role model to me, not only because of his successful career but also because of his love for music and his ability to connect with people. With his high-paying job and extensive networking, he had access to opportunities that were rare in our lower-income community, and he used his influence to help others whenever he could.

In addition to his professional accomplishments, Jose had a passion for music that he shared with me from a young age. I remember him introducing me to rock, metal, heavy metal, and screamo music, and encouraging me to play several low-brass instruments. His enthusiasm for music was contagious, and it inspired me to pursue my own creative interests.

But what I admired most about my uncle was his authenticity and his willingness to be open and honest with others. He never pretended to be someone he wasn't, and he encouraged me to do the same. I always felt comfortable being myself around him, knowing that he would never judge me for who I was. He even bought me my first skateboard, recognizing and supporting my interests even when others might have seen them as unconventional.

However, despite our strong connection, we did have our disagreements. I was never afraid to ask him tough questions or challenge his opinions, and sometimes this led to heated debates. But even when we didn't see eye to eye, I knew that my uncle valued my honesty and respected my opinions. He was a constant source of inspiration and support in my life, and I will always be grateful for the impact he had on me. You see, Jose had a really good job and made over $100k a year in the early 2000s, so he had nice things and he also had connections/networking. He often knew some "higher-up" people in the San Antonio – Dallas, TX area, and for people like me, who are in the lower poverty area – that meant something.

We were proud of Jose and all the great things he was doing with his life because of his career choices and advances. Able was no "figure" in my life, Jose was.

He also inspired me to be forward and up-front with people. It makes interactions and communication better and more open than feeling like you are hiding who you really are. I could be myself around him and not feel like he would say something sideways about how I did something. I loved that about my uncle and he loved my personality, but where we clashed was my questions:

"Why is Viky like this? She makes me feel like I am crazy! Everything is HER HER HER! If she has a bad day at work, who gets yelled at, ME! You, Able, Valeria, and Martha get to leave! I HAVE TO STAY HERE! I HAVE NO WHERE TO ESCAPE TO! WHY does Viky do this to me?"

The response was always:

"You know mom loves you, she does these things

31

because she loves you and doesn't want you out on the streets."

That statement will be the darkest statement I had heard in a while. It took the cake for me, **she does these things because SHE LOVES YOU, <u>BECAUSE SHE LOVES ME</u>**? I'd rather be shot to death execution-style than hear that fucking bullshit again from Jose. I would just agree with him to get it over with and stop talking about Viky. I loved Jose very much and didn't want to upset him with things involving Viky. I guess he either was blindsided or was used to this kind of behavior or maybe he knew and didn't want to face how she was. Many people would do this to either reshape reality in their heads or make it into one that is more manageable for them in their heads.

Then there's my paternal aunt, Valeria. Mama's girl. Valeria has an interesting way of living her life. She was the FAKEST person I had ever known. She often showed me her chats online, where she was catfishing men; who had no idea what was going on. I knew she was discussing "adult" things when she would pull her laptop away from my sight or tell me to leave the bedroom because we shared a bedroom together. Very weird she was no doubt but looking at it from an adult perspective it really does get fucked up when you are not in control, and you give in to your worst issues.

We were both large, fat, people trying to squeeze onto a queen-size bed that we DID NOT FIT ON. I often had to sleep on my left side up against the wall so that we could fit but often were squished or pushed up against the window because Valeria would roll over onto me. We were too fat for that bed.

Sigh, then there is my stepmother, Martha. I used to put so much blame on her for my father's negligent behavior but later found out that most of it was all him. Martha often offered to include me in her family events but Able did not want me there. Martha often took many tongue-lashings from me about how she took Able away from me to raise her two sons, but it was all to protect Able. My stepmother knew the truth and did what she could to include me while Able would tell me it was because I was a girl and he never knew when I was "on the rag".

I will never forget when a cousin committed suicide, and classmate of mine, passed away in the early 2000s from medical issues. Martha was there, holding me like a mother, and was not telling me to suck it up the way my father would tell me to when I would cry. Martha made it safe for me in a moment of weakness and heartache.

I will never be able to tell Martha how sorry I am for

treating her the way that I did as a child (and saying I didn't know better is not a valid excuse, either).

Martha, if you read this book and have figured out this is "you", I'm sorry for all the mean and hurtful things I said to you in the 14 years I knew you. I know it may be too late now, but just know that this apology is truthful and honest. I hope you are living a very happy and fulfilled life, Martha. I love you and miss you.

Now, let's jump back to Viky, as things weren't always bad with her because there was a short time when things were okay. Life was normal for a few years or so throughout my life. It often felt like she gaslighted Lupe and me about being in a good mood. We would have periods of where she was overtly happy and really enjoyable. Viky would not yell, she would cook dinner at home (we would eat out a lot at the local Whataburger), and she'd even lay off all the mean names she'd call me in reference to my mother, Mila.

Some days, during these moments of happiness, but just like most moments in life it was a fleeting moment because happiness is just a moment before you need more happiness.

We would go out into the town and if I said, I liked

something she would just buy it and not yell at me for mentioning I liked something. I could often find her staring at me in the house from the kitchen table just in a deep stare, almost lost in her mind, but as soon as I moved, she would ask me what I was doing or ask me where I was going. I often felt like maybe she had some really bad undiagnosed mental illness but that didn't give her the right to treat me badly when she did.

Here is where things get wild and crazy, enter my maternal-grandfather, Hugo. He is the wild one on my moms' side of the family. The head "wild-man" of the family, and we love him so much for his wild and carefree spirit.

Hugo was reputably known for being a ladies' man in his time in our small town, but when he met his ex-wife, Carmen, he had most of his family with her. My mother came from this marriage along with my aunt, Nataly (Lily), and uncle, HJ (for Hugo Jr). My maternal-grandfather was a carpenter and looked a lot like an old western cartoon-cowboy from back in the day with his long handle-bar mustache, and standing no taller than 4' 11''; he is a firecracker and a hell-of-a carpenter. His mind can create things that he can transfer onto wood; it's just amazing.

My second mother, my tia Nataly, Lily, you by far were and still are the best person in my life.

You have been there no matter what and have always made sure I knew as much of the truth about Able and Mila as possible. Even when I called you mom and you corrected me and reminded me that Mila was my mother; I still appreciate that today. I know that Viky tried to keep me from you and the family, especially Mila.

I was scared to death when I found out you had skin cancer and I am so happy that you fought the hardest fight of all and you are still here today kicking and screaming! I love you tia!

Let's not forget my best-friend, Teresa, Ter-Beri! I have known Teri for most of my life and how we became friends was a very interesting story: She was dating my older cousin when I was 12 and we bonded over video games. At first, like most awesome friendships, they begin with y'all not liking each other, and well, that was exactly how it was in our case. Since my older cousin was in a situation where his grandmother dictated a lot of his life, I was always the third wheel for them. I was like a little sister to my older cousin, but the dynamic between us wasn't fair to him. I bullied my older cousin because it was a reflection of what was happening at my home, so Teri didn't like that and hated me for it. (Bro, if you know this is you, I AM SO SORRY I had bullied you over the years. I know it's no excuse, but again I am super sorry for being that way to you all those years). So, having the protective nature she did she stood up for my older cousin and we both clashed because of this. Shortly after Teri and my cousin broke up Teri and I became friends because we no longer had my older cousin "in between us". Our friendship opened up and was amazing after that.

Teri is about 7 years my senior and our dynamic is just amazing. Teri has allowed me to be as open about my emotions, personality, and be the strangest person I can be. We would take long drives down in the back roads of my home town blasting music and dancing in the car. We even sat at the local park and sang our hearts out in her car or ate ice cream and "spilling the tea" about current events in our lives. We never got into trouble when we were together and I loved that about Teri. She was always a safe place/person for me. She was there, first hand for a lot of things that people had no idea about. She has been there for the abuse (actually witnessed me being physically abused by Viky), the put-downs (by Able), and she's even been there for me in ways I cannot explain.

EARNING A RIBBON

Memory:

It was a normal summer night, and I had been out with Teri at the movie theater in the next few towns over (45 minute drive one-way). We were having the best time walking around the superstore in that area when I get a call on my cell phone about how I need to come home already.
"HIJA DE LA CHINGA, WHERE ARE YOU?!", Viky said on the other side of the phone nearly blowing out the speakers.

"I am still with Teri. The movie let out about 10 minutes ago and we decided to come to the superstore so Teri can get a gas card to put gas in her car", I say nervously. My whole body is shaking and trembling from the anxiety that's building from the phone call.
"Vas a ver werka! (You'll see, child!)", she's nearly hissing at this point, "If you don't come home soon then you'll really see what pissed off looks like."
I hang up the phone and turn to Teri, "I have to go home already. My grandma is mad and I can't stay out any longer. Lets get the gas and go, please."

So we continue on the awkward 45 minute drive back home. We are about 5 minutes from my grandparents home when my phone rings again and its my grandma, "DONDE

ESTAS!! (WHERE ARE YOU?!)", she's screaming now. I tell her I am almost home and Teri looks over at me and says, "I'm staying the night. I can't let you go home like this." I looked at Teri nervous and didn't know what she had planned but she came inside the home with me when we got there. Viky was not happy to see Teri there with me as she knew something was up. "Fold the clothes," she said walking past me quickly and not looking at me. I grabbed all the clothes in a big bear hug and walked with it to the living room from the kitchen area. Teri sat next to me to help and I put my hand out to stop her and shook my head no. I continued to fold the clothes as Teri sat there on the floor watching me. I eventually finish, I pick up all the clothes and towels so that I take them to their respective rooms. As I am finishing I hear Viky in the bathroom going through the closet looking at the towels I just folded. She begins to pull all of the towels, bedding, and linens out of the closet and says, "YOU DIDN'T DO THIS RIGHT! YOU DID IT IN A HURRY BECAUSE YOUR LITTLE FRIEND IS HERE!! FIX! IT!" I'm now standing in the door way of the restroom staring at her in awe because she hadn't ever had a "moment" like this before that day. She grabbed me by the arm into the restroom and grabbed a wire hanger that was in the closet and began hitting me with it on my arms, shoulders, and back. "Wait, owe! Wait!," I say as she's hitting me. I pit up my hands in defense, "Put. Your. Hands. Down. Or. Its. Going. To. Be. Worse.," she says with every swing. I can hear the wire hanger whistling in the air while she's hitting me. It sounds like the silence screams I thought were coming out of my mouth, but Teri heard me down the hallway and came running, "STOP! STOP OR I'M CALLING THE COPS!" The room got silent. I suddenly couldn't feel the stinging licks from the hanger anymore. I was crying. Broken and distressed. OVER TOWELS.

Viky stood there and finally said, "Teri, it's time for you to go." Teri looked at me in horror as I signaled to her to leave. I gave her a look that said *"I'll be okay"*, and she left. Later that night I got punished some more for there being a witness to her wrong doing.

Back to Teri, I never knew a person like her could even exist when I first met her but we have had our fall-outs and come-back together moments but every time it happens, I go out of my way to make sure I have my friend back in my life. She's the sister I never had. We even made a little slogan for ourselves:

"Best friend

noun

The ass to my crack,

the cheese to my mac,

the main bitch who always has my back"

Teri has also been there for my slips in my mental health. She's been the main support system for staying on track with my mental health. She knows when I am not "myself" or if there are days I go without talking to her I get a *"Where you at?"* text; just to make sure I'm still alive, haha! I am very thankful and appreciative of my best friend for always being there for me and opening up my eyes to what freedom of life and expression feels like. Teri and I have been through a lot together. We've had our fair share of arguments, misunderstandings, and disagreements, but we always manage to find our way back to each other. One thing that I love about our friendship is that we are able to be completely honest with each other, even if it's something that the other person may not want to hear. It's not always easy, but it's necessary for our growth as individuals and as friends.

When I first started experiencing mental health issues, I was scared to talk about it with anyone. I didn't want people to think that I was weak or crazy. But Teri was different. She listened to me without judgment and helped me find resources for therapy and medication.

Having someone like Teri in my life has been a game-changer. She reminds me to take my medication, encourages me to go to therapy, and checks in on me regularly to make sure that I'm doing okay. I don't know where I'd be without her. Thank you, bestie! I love you!

Last but not least, my paternal grandfather, Lupe, he was the best man I had ever known. He's a Vietnam Veteran and has a heart of gold. He truly showed me what to look for and what not to look for in a man. I can't imagine what/how my life would be without him in my upbringing. He showed me how to survive off the land, track wild animals, find my sense of direction by looking up at the sky and trees, and he even showed me how to skin whatever I have hunted. Lupe was very active in my life and upbringing. He often worked long and stressful hours as a hunting guide at a ranch 45 minutes from my hometown; when he came home, he always asked how I was or what I did at school. Sometimes, we'd sit outside and just talk about what new books I'd read or what I'd learned in school.

Lupe had a special way of making me feel seen and heard. He would always take the time to listen to me and answer my questions, no matter how silly or insignificant they may have seemed. He had a wealth of knowledge and experience that he was more than willing to share with me, and I cherished every moment I spent with him.

One of my fondest memories with Lupe was when he took me on a hunting trip for the first time. I was only 10 years old, and I had never been hunting before. I was nervous and unsure of what to expect, but Lupe was patient and reassuring. He showed me how to use the rifle properly and how to track animals. He taught me to respect nature and the animals that we hunted.

We spent the whole day out in the wilderness, and even though we didn't catch anything, it was one of the best days of my life. We talked and laughed and enjoyed each other's company. I felt so alive and connected to nature. I'll never forget that day, and I'll always be grateful to Lupe for showing me that side of life.

He was very proud of me for being in the marching and symphonic band throughout my years in school and was even more proud of how successful I was in Horticulture and Agriculture through my 4-H group. Lupe always told everyone bout my accomplishments and what I was succeeding in because he often told me how much he loved

43

and cherished me.

When I questioned my existence in front of him, he often reminded me that when I was born that was the happiest day of his life. So, when I was with Lupe, I always felt love and happiness from/around him. His hugs had always been the best and the most welcoming thing in my life that I had ever felt. When things were hard, I always had him to turn to, but then when the day came that I had to leave home, that's when things changed between us. I still love my paternal grandfather very much and wish him the best life he can live. I think of him often, and am grateful for the lessons he has taught me throughout the years. Growing up, my grandfather was always there to offer advice, support and guidance. He was a hardworking man who instilled in me the importance of family values and responsibility. He taught me to appreciate the small things in life and to never take anything for granted. I fondly remember the many times he took me fishing, and the stories he shared with me while we sat around the campfire.

Above all, he taught me to always love unconditionally, and that is something I will never forget. My grandfather has seen me through some of life's toughest challenges, and for that I will be forever thankful. I am blessed to have had such an amazing person in my life, and

I hope to be able to repay him in some way for all of his kindness and wisdom. Wishing my grandfather health, happiness and peace in his life. I will always love you grandpa. No matter what.

In conclusion, I am blessed to have had such amazing people in my life who have shaped me into the person I am today. My mother taught me strength and resilience, my best friend taught me the importance of self-expression and mental health, and my grandfather taught me the value of hard work, respect, and living in harmony with nature. I owe them all a debt of gratitude that I can never repay, but I will always cherish them and hold them close to my heart.

Chapter 3: A Moment in Time

"This chapter will go into my coming of age. I will lay the bare-naked truth about what occurred, not holding back on anything."

"A moment in time" refers to a single moment that holds significance or importance in someone's life. It can be a moment of joy, sorrow, inspiration, or reflection that can stay with a person for the rest of their life. In this chapter, we will discuss what a moment in time is, how it can impact someone's life, and how to appreciate and cherish these moments.

A moment in time can be a fleeting experience that occurs in a matter of seconds or a more prolonged experience that lasts for minutes, hours, or even days. It can be a moment of intense emotion, such as the birth of a child, the death of a loved one, or the achievement of a long-awaited goal. It can also be a simple moment of reflection, such as watching a beautiful sunset, listening to a piece of music that touches the heart, or being struck by the beauty of nature.

These moments can have a profound impact on a person's life, shaping their identity, values, and beliefs. They can serve as reminders of the importance of living in the present moment, cherishing life's little pleasures, and making the most of the time we have. They can also provide a sense of perspective, helping us to understand our place in the world and the impact we can have on those around us.

However, it's important to remember that a moment in time is subjective and can mean different things to different people. What may be a significant moment for one person may not hold the same significance for another. For example, a person's first kiss may be a momentous occasion for them, while another person may not attach the same significance to it. Similarly, a person may find meaning in a moment of quiet contemplation, while another may find significance in a more outwardly dramatic experience.

One way to appreciate and cherish these moments is to live in the present moment and be fully present in the experience. This means letting go of distractions and worries, focusing on what is happening around you, and fully engaging with the experience. It's also important to be open to new experiences, to seek out moments that are meaningful and significant, and to take risks that allow you to grow and learn.

Another way to appreciate and cherish these moments is to document them in some way. This can be through journaling, taking photographs, or creating artwork that captures the essence of the moment. By recording these moments, we can revisit them and relive the emotions and experiences associated with them, allowing us to appreciate them even more deeply.

It's also important to remember that moments in time can be both positive and negative. While we may naturally want to hold onto positive moments and cherish them, it's important to also acknowledge and process negative moments. These moments can be opportunities for growth and learning, and can teach us valuable lessons about ourselves and the world around us.

In conclusion, a moment in time is a significant moment that holds meaning and significance in someone's life. It can be a moment of joy, sorrow, reflection, or inspiration that can shape a person's identity, values, and beliefs. By living in the present moment, documenting these experiences, and acknowledging both positive and negative moments, we can fully appreciate and cherish the moments in time that make life so rich and meaningful.

Life is like a river, constantly flowing and changing

as it moves through time. Each moment is a unique blend of experiences, thoughts, and emotions, like a collection of individual water droplets that together make up the river's current. Imagine standing on the bank of this river, watching as the water rushes past you. In one moment, you may feel a sense of calm as the river flows gently and steadily, like a smooth and peaceful melody. But in the next moment, the current may pick up speed and intensity, crashing against rocks and creating a tumultuous and chaotic sound. As you stand there, observing the ebb and flow of the river, you realize that each moment is fleeting and unique, just like the water droplets that make up the current. Some moments may be peaceful and serene, while others may be challenging and tumultuous. But no matter what, each moment is a part of the greater whole, contributing to the constantly evolving journey of life.

Sometimes, we may wish to hold onto certain moments in life, like trying to grasp a handful of water from the river. But just like the water slipping through our fingers, these moments too will inevitably slip away. It's important to cherish each moment, to fully experience it, and then let it go, allowing the current of life to carry us forward.

As we continue to flow with the current of life, we may encounter obstacles and challenges, much like the river's rapids and rocks. But just like the river flows around these obstacles, we too must find ways to navigate through the challenges that come our way.

Ultimately, as we continue to move forward on our journey, we may not know exactly where the river of life is taking us. But by embracing each moment and trusting in the journey, we can find meaning and purpose in the flow of life, just like how each droplet of water contributes to the river's path and destination.

High school can be a great place where you get to have new experiences and meet different people. It should be a joyous time in any teenager's life, but there are many who don't experience that in fact they experience the complete opposite. Sadly, I am one of those people.

Even though many people say that the bad times pass and as you grow older you will look back at it and laugh. Some people may even suggest that you will forget about time and that those moments dissipate like rain following onto the ground. As for me, I remember it like it was yesterday, I was fourteen years old, and going through a lot at home as it is but then a bolder is dropped on you by people that are supposed to mentor you during this crucial period. My coach, whom I looked up to, takes one look at me and without hesitation calls me 'fat' after coming back from the summer break. That moment in time stuck with me throughout my adult life.

You would think "This must be the worst of it" But sadly my life wasn't going to get easier as being 210 pounds at the age of 14 was simply unacceptable, I guess. I was being bullied constantly from all quarters of the school and even though I was taking part in numerous different school-based activities such as sports and whatnot, then the cloud of depression the dark passenger in my life crept up as I started to hate being at school and didn't want to be there as the bullying created a lack of self-confidence and then the problems at home was becoming too much.

Kids who are regularly targeted by bullies frequently suffer both emotionally and socially. Not only do they find it hard to make friends, but they also struggle to maintain healthy friendships.

Being bullied is an unfortunately common problem in school. It can affect all ages, from elementary to high school, and from all quarters of the school. It can be verbal, physical, or even digital. I experienced all three during my time in school. It was a constant struggle to make it through each day and I felt like I was being attacked from all angles.

I eventually had to take drastic steps to protect myself and stand up for myself. The first step was to talk to a trusted adult, whether that was a teacher, guidance counselor, or even a parent. This adult can then help you work out a plan to deal with the bully and make sure they are held accountable for their actions. You can also choose to talk to your peers and try to get them on your side. Lastly, you can report the bullying to the authorities and seek legal action if necessary. No matter what you decide to do, it's important that you take control of the situation and stand up for yourself against the bully.

Part of this struggle is directly related to low self-regard. A lack of self-regard is a direct result of the mean and hurtful effects that other kids say about them. When children are continually called "fat" or "disasters," they begin to believe these effects are true.

Bullying victims also tend to witness a wide range of feelings. They may feel angry, bitter, vulnerable, helpless, frustrated, lonely, and insulated from their peers. Accordingly, they may skip classes and resort to medicines and alcohol to numb their pain. And if bullying is on-going, they may develop depression and indeed contemplate suicide.

There's no single cause of depression, according to exploration. Brain chemistry, hormones, genetics, life experiences, and physical health can all play a part.

Still, ultimately kids can develop what's known as "learned helplessness". If no intervention takes place. Learned helplessness means that the targets of bullying believe that they cannot do anything to change the situation. As a result, they stop trying also, the cycle down into depression becomes more severe. This leads to a feeling of forlornness and the belief that there's no way out.

As bullied kids grow into grown-ups, they may continue to struggle with self-regard, have difficulty developing and maintaining connections, and avoid social relations. They also may have a hard time trusting people, which can impact their particular connections and their work connections.

They may indeed start to believe falsehoods about bullying, such as persuading themselves that the bullying was not as bad as they remember. They also may engage in self-blame.

Kids who are bullied frequently suffer academically, too. Bullied kids struggle to concentrate on their practice. In fact, slipping grades is one of the first signs that a child is being bullied. Children also may be so preoccupied with bullying that they forget about assignments or have difficulty paying attention in class.

Also, bullied kids may skip school or classes in order to avoid being bullied. This practice also can affect falling grades. And when grades begin to drop this adds to the stressful situations the bullied child is formerly passing.

One possible reason for the lower scores in schools with pervasive bullying is that students are frequently less engaged in the literacy process because they're too detracted by or upset about the bullying. also, instructors may be less effective because they must spend so important time concentrated on classroom operation and discipline rather than tutoring. The good news is with proper support and intervention, most children targeted by bullies will overcome bullying and the effects will get back to normal. But left unchecked, bullying can beget the victim to pay a high cost in long-term consequences.

When a child is bullied, it isn't uncommon for the parents and siblings to also be affected. Parents frequently witness a wide range of consequences including feeling helpless to fix the situation. They also may feel alone and insulated. And they may indeed come hung up with the situation frequently at the expense of their own health and good.

My paternal uncle Jose was someone who supported me and was one of the only few people who came to my aid by suggesting me a diet which I thought would help me as I started losing weight. It's weird you think you have life figured out and that you know the right pathway but life is not what you intend it to be and how it pans out. I did start to lose weight and feel better at the start because I thought this was the path way towards discovering myself again to be happy again but as time passed this diet, which I thought was going to give me a healthy pathway towards a normal life, turned on me. I became obsessive about losing weight so much so my intake was less than the minimum requirement of what a child should have. This again comes down to the society we are living in that wants you to be a certain way to accept you which is very similar to how I was being treated at home where I had to pretend to be someone I am not. Anyway, time passed and I did lose weight but at the cost of my sanity and physical health which led to me passing out and vomiting blood. When I came to and opened my eyes, I had two IVs in my arm and the doctor revealing to me that I had passed out due to malnutrition and that I needed to stop my diet.

After this had happened, I was diagnosed with a disease called Helicobacter pylori, and now I have to change my eating habits and instead of moving forward and getting control of my life I instead was pulled back in. So, my junior year was just me making costly mistakes an learning from them. I then helped the children in the agriculture group I was in to help children learn how to take care of animals. This was a turning point as I was learning leadership skills that helped me get my confidence back and I in fact graduated with honors!

I was part of the symphonic/marching band and during our graduation ceremony I request to be on stage and that is when something happened that still makes me shiver, I heard a voice, a voice that I didn't think I would hear on that day. It was my mom who called out my name. "GO MARISSA!" I could feel my heart in my throat.

After the graduation ceremony ended, I could not wait to get to her, I even didn't talk to my friends about the graduation and instead just went towards her as she was waiting for me by the gate at the end of the bleachers.

As I was making my way toward her my father stopped me and told me not to believe what she says and not to fall for her lies. I didn't care at that moment and simply said "Yeah, sure whatever".

I kept walking and stood right in front of her. We didn't hug, shake hands, or don't anything, we just stood there staring at each other, with extreme glee and happiness not knowing how to react. It was a moment in time that could have lasted an eternity. I had not seen in her about 10 years and I had so much that I wanted to say to her but I just didn't know how or what to say, I wanted to tell her how angry I was she wasn't there in my life and what I had to go through because she wasn't there. They say that even when you grow up and become a mature adult you are simply hiding that child within you, this was exactly what I was feeling, I felt like a kid again.

I had to say something but when I saw her, she said three simple words, five words that I have been waiting to hear for years "I am proud of you" At this moment I didn't know what to say in response, and I did the only thing that made sense at the time, I accepted her and embraced her.

This moment was what you would call the end of a long pursuit of happiness. Ever since I was a child, I had been searching for contentment and joy in life. I had tried different paths, from academic achievement and career success to material pleasures and experiences. But nothing seemed to bring the kind of lasting happiness that I hoped for. My mother's hugs were a source of comfort and light in the darkness of my existence. Growing up, I often felt isolated and alone, struggling to make sense of the world around me. No matter how hard life got, I could always imagine her embrace for warmth and courage. No words were ever necessary - as she was a symbol and I could feel her unconditional love, a reminder that I would never be alone. My mother's hug was a ray of sunshine that illuminated the darkness in my life. Her hugs were an anchor to keep me grounded, and a reminder that no matter what happened, we were connected by an unbreakable bond of love, sadly though my grandmother arrived saying the ugliest things about my mom who had to leave because she didn't want to ruin my night.

I couldn't quite understand why she was suddenly so angry with her. I knew that my mom had done nothing wrong, but my grandmother's harsh words still hurt.

I will end this chapter with a quote that I love *"There's a story behind everything. How a picture got on a wall. How a scar got on your face. Sometimes the stories are simple, and sometimes they are hard and heartbreaking. But behind all your stories is always your mother's story, because hers is where yours begin."* - Mitch Albom

Chapter 4: Too Soon

"This is the chapter when I lost more than I thought I ever could. It all happened fast and it all happened too soon"

Losing a loved one too soon is a difficult experience that no one should ever have to go through. It can be especially difficult when there is no warning or time to prepare for leaving family and friends and being unable to say a proper goodbye. Grief can be overwhelming and all-consuming, bringing forth a wave of intense emotions – sadness, anger, guilt, confusion – and often a feeling of helplessness. It can be hard to understand why this happened and accept the situation's finality. Finding a way to cope with the grief is key in order to beginning the healing process. Talking to friends and family, seeking professional help, and engaging in self-care activities are all important steps that can help you through this trying time. It's also important to remember that it's ok to feel what you're feeling, no matter how difficult it may feel. By allowing yourself to experience the emotions, you can ultimately find peace in the memories you have and the fact that your loved one will always be remembered.

Life can be a beautiful lie. We think we have all the time in the world, and we think we can always get the closure that we always need but sometimes life isn't just like that. You think you are going to grow old together with your loved ones forever but the truth is that it is just fantasy and something we tell ourselves, a beautiful lie.

Losing a loved one too soon can have a profound and lasting impact on one's life. When someone we love passes away, we often experience a range of intense emotions that can be difficult to process. These emotions may include sadness, anger, guilt, confusion, and helplessness, to name a few. It's natural to feel overwhelmed by these feelings, but it's important to remember that they are a normal and expected part of the grieving process.

One of the most challenging aspects of losing a loved one suddenly is the lack of warning or time to prepare. It can be difficult to come to terms with the finality of the situation and accept that our loved one is no longer with us.

It was a regular night, I remember having dinner at the table, I was about to finish my dinner when I saw my grandparents listening to something. My maternal grandfathers' name, Hugo, come up on the police scanner that they owned. Something bad had happened and I feared the worst as it was a "code 500" which meant there was a dead body involved. Viky came to me and informed me that she and Valeria were going to my mother's trailer to see if everything was okay. My heart skipped a beat a few times in that moment and I could feel the food in front of me smell sour under my nose. I told them that I would be staying at home, thinking that it might be an immigrant as it was not too uncommon in that area. My paternal grandmother and aunt left.

They had been gone for around 45 minutes but for me it felt like an eternity. I lay in my bed string at the wall just thinking of all the things that could have possibly happened, but I wanted to believe that whatever it was could not be my mother being the code 500. I couldn't fathom that thought, and the more I thought about it the more I felt ill to my stomach. They came back and told me there was an ambulance, police and the fire department that were not allowing them to pass, but I declined thinking about how my stepfather could have beaten up my mother really bad one last time but as fate would have it, I got a call from my moms' sister, Nataly, that I needed to come to the hospital which was more an hour away. I suddenly felt my whole insides shake, my teeth began to chatter as anxiety took over,

I stood from my bed and paced back and forth as I spoke to my aunt Nataly, and all I could hear inside my head was,

"Please God, don't take my mother from me!"

They told me that they had taken my mom by helicopter to the hospital because it was a severe head injury. I clenched my teeth so tight I felt the porcelain bridge inside my lower jaw break apart in my mouth. I spit out some of the pieces into my hand and place them in a napkin I had nearby.

I stood there in my bedroom, alone, and stared at the wall for 15 minutes contemplating what I had just been told, and it was only until Lupe came to me and told me that I needed to go, I snapped out of it and grabbed my bag and got into the car with my paternal grandparents and went to the hospital. During that ride I can't tell you much, I barely remember that car ride, but I do remember seeing the lines in the road passing by through the window as I blasted my *Three Day Grace: One X* album over my iPod. When we arrived there and I ran to the reception desk frantic, the receptionist was trying to verify who I was when my family members heard me, I was loud enough that they could hear me through the halls of the hospital. They quickly came and got me. I ran as fast as I could fearing the worst, it was an experience that I had never had before, it was like an out-of-body experience where I didn't know if it was real or not. I reached the intensive care unit and saw my other relatives trying to see my mother. As I got there one of my relatives, in shock, said

"ES UN ESPIRITU!"/ "It's a ghost!"

Since I was a spitting image of my mother, and someone said, "No that is her oldest daughter, Marissa."

My mother had me when she was 15 so the realization for everyone was setting in along with the tragic event that had unfolded. The eyes and whispers began as I passed up the crowd of people huddled around the double doors.

I made my way into the ICU, the nurses tried to approach me but I walked past them and what I saw was something I could never forget. My mother whom I loved from the bottom of my heart, had tubes in and around her, her body was covered but her head wasn't. I gasped and grabbed my face with both of my hands and heard Hugo say,

"Oh, no. I'm so sorry mija".

I fell to my knees and sat there in shock for a minute. I saw the nurses coming once again and I immediately stood up and said,

"DON'T. TOUCH. ME."

I could see everything, I saw her skull was exposed but there were large staples over the giant gash in her head, they had her hooked up to the life support machine because she wasn't responding to tests they had performed on her in the helicopter. I grabbed her hand telling her

"Mom it's me, I am here",

I was trying to hold in my tears and sobs. I felt so helpless! I wanted to scream out from the horrible pain I was feeling inside.

She squeezed my hand back and gave me a little hope that maybe she could make it through this; I was going to stay by her side no matter what. My maternal grandmother, and two sisters were standing beside her in tears; I had never seen this strong woman ever cry, and that made it harder for the rest of us to keep it together emotionally. About 15 minutes later the doctor came in to tell us that they were going to unhook her from life support to see whether she could breathe on her own. Then the moment he told us that there was no brain activity my heart was shattered once over again, now in a trillion little pieces, because I knew it was over. They unhooked the life support machine, and she started to take her last breaths, I remember her hands going cold as she slowly faded away. That was it, she went, and just like that it was over. My ears were ringing so loud I couldn't hear a word or sound around me. I felt like my heart was shattering a million times over and over again inside my chest.

This was something no child should see, something that scars us for life. There are things in life that I contemplate about, things that I can't fathom. To see your loved one like this makes the love you had for them become poison in your veins, the uncontrollable mental anguish sometimes makes you wish you yourself never existed so you are spared your pain.

Imagine the most psychologically painful thing that you have ever endured. Actually, take a moment and do it. As you do that, realize that all it took for you to readdress it was a dozen written words from a person you have likely no way met. That is how close to your life that pain you just felt still is and always will be. Loss is painful. That is the trouble.

Take the loss of someone you love. The sense of having lost someone or something, without any hope of recovering it, requires a profoundly different approach than jerking back from a hot pan. But the challenge it presents is clearer and further inarguable It's not exceptional. You'll go to your grave just many words down from nearly any notable pain or loss you have ever endured. Anytime, anywhere, mortal cognition can bring it back. Mental relations and memory are like that.

When a loved one dies, the loss follows you from room to room, moment to moment. It's both endless and ever-present. Although we know that loss isn't going down, there are those eons of mortal practice in trying to avoid pain. We foolishly engage that heritage indeed with the loss of those we love.

We may try not to lament the death or distract ourselves with other tasks — hoping against that thinking of something differently will dwindle the pain. We may directly try to suppress a sense of sadness. We avoid allowing of sweet moments with the loved one, allured into repression of our memory by the deceptively soothing short-term effect. We may pretend the loss didn't do or deny its counteraccusations — refusing to ever alter a loved one's bedroom, as if she or he'll return to reclaim it. Repression and avoidance come at a high cost — they dwindle our capability to do much of anything differently. The trouble to suppress and run down is exhausting and ultimately fails. Always, the painful reality of the loss returns. Pain doesn't really vanish when suppressed or avoided; it's right there, under the face. Avoidance does not make sadness lower of a problem; it makes it further of a problem because you have to keep working harder and harder to suppress it.

Back at the hospital, I walked out of the doors so that I could find my paternal grandparents, there were nowhere to be seen until my relatives told me that they were in the waiting room. I went into the waiting room and came back out, I couldn't find them or that's what I thought I was experiencing, but then something happened. It was like the floodgates were opened and I started to cry my heart out, I began wailing in a corner of the hospital tucked away into myself in the fetal position – rocking back and forth - it was something I had no control over, the nurses came and tried to calm me down but to no avail so they took me to a room and sedated me. The ordeal broke me completely, the next day, I awoke and said nothing, then I went back home.

We held a wake for my mother to which everyone showed up, the entire town including the people from my high school, and relatives who I hadn't even met. One of them was an uncle from my mother's side, it wasn't the way I would have wanted to meet him but I was just so lost in my pain and thoughts, and her getting buried was like seeing myself get buried – I felt like my soul was leaving me and holding onto my mothers' casket as I watched her get lowered into the ground. It was almost like everything went silent inside my heart and suddenly became hardened with pain and darkness – and I started to think about what could have been. All the years we could have had together, all the time we could have spent together was suddenly ripped away from me when I could finally see a life with my mother, it all went through my mind.

As people left and said their condolences and goodbyes, I stood there at the foot of her gave for a few minutes and thought about all the cruel things I had said to her over the years. I know we had made amends at my middle sister's 16th birthday party but deep down inside I was still very broken up by all the hurtful things I had said and done. All I could think about was how I was going to find the truth out about what really happened with my mom and dad.

My first memory of my mother was when I was about 4 or 5 years old and it was during the time I was at my great-grandmother's house. This was the time my mother had visiting rights and I was numb. The shock of my mother's death had not yet sunk in, and it felt like I was watching the scene unfold from a distance. I had always known that my mother was in an abusive relationship, but I never thought it would come to this. My mother had always been my protector, my rock, and now she was gone.

As I sat alone in Viky's home, I felt a deep sense of despair. I had never felt so alone in my life. The house was eerily quiet, and every corner reminded me of my mother's presence.

My mind was a whirlwind of emotions. I was angry, confused, and overwhelmed all at once. How could my mother's partner do this to her? How could someone who claimed to love my mother hurt her in such a brutal way? I was angry at myself for not doing more to help her mother, and for not recognizing the signs of abuse sooner. Maybe if we had been together more, I could have prevented this tragedy.

I was overwhelmed by the realization that I would never be able to make it up to my mother, never be able to tell her how sorry I was.

My grief was all-encompassing. I couldn't eat, sleep, or concentrate on anything. All I could think about was my mother, and the fact that she was gone forever. The days and weeks after my mother's death were a blur. I felt like she was going through the motions of life, but nothing felt real. I was haunted by memories of my mother, both good and bad, and it was impossible to escape the overwhelming sense of loss.

In the midst of my grief, I was also struggling with feelings of abandonment. I felt like my entire world had been turned upside down, and I didn't know who to trust anymore. How could someone who claimed to love my mother do something so terrible? I was struggling to come to terms with the fact that the man my mother had loved had also been the one to take her life.

As time went on, I began to realize that my mother's death had changed me in fundamental ways. I was no longer the carefree, happy-go-lucky girl I used to be. The trauma of losing my mother had left a permanent scar on my psyche. I was now more guarded, less trusting of others, and more aware of the darkness that existed in the world. I knew that I would never be the same again and that my mother's death would continue to affect me for the rest of my life.

Despite the pain and sorrow that I felt, I also knew that I had to find a way to move forward. My mother would have wanted me to live a happy, fulfilling life, and I didn't want to disappoint her memory.

One of the most accessible things I had in my life was

alcohol. I used to go to parties in barns and enjoyed myself but it was more because of what was going on in my home. This became even more so after the loss of my mother, I had stopped giving a shit about my life as I didn't pay attention to what I was eating and as I was in college I stopped going to class and fell into a deep dark hole of sadness and trauma. Knowing the fact that my step father was out there free even after what he did to my mother was something I couldn't get over. I was also fearful of the fact that he might come back and do the same to me as he did to my mother because when I lived with them or visited he let me know every chance he got to remind me that I wasn't his real child and that he can do whatever he wanted to me. My mind was fully wrapped with anger, guilt, and fear. He always threatened me and my father's family by saying stuff like *"I will burn down the house with all of you inside"* Among other things, so this fear was always at the forefront of my mind.

When he was on the run, he ended up in Michigan and got caught there. He had family in Michigan but he made a fatal mistake when he checked himself in the hospital and tried to get medicine, it was there he realized that there was a manhunt for him. He then went to a store where the cashier recognized my stepfather since the cashier had seen him on the news. The cashier then cleverly told my stepfather to wait since he had to check his id and instead contacted the police who came and captured him.

From there he was then extradited to Texas and spent time in jail until his court date. They set his bond for 500,000 dollars with a condition that he would have to wear an ankle monitor. His father somehow came up with the money and posted bail for him. My stepfather got the ankle monitor but as soon as he got back to his mother's house he cut off his ankle monitor and buried it in his mother's backyard so that the authorities would think he was at home where he was supposed to be. He was put on America's Top 10 Most Wanted list, by a grand-aunt on my maternal side who is a lawyer (she reached out to the Texas Rangers because the local authorities weren't doing enough to catch my stepfather), and was always a danger to whomever he met.

He then went on the run but this time he ran away for 4 years and was actually found in Mexico where the good people there came together to help get him captured. During this time, I had moved out of Texas to North Carolina with my then-boyfriend and now husband, and I was living in fear because knowing he had people in Michigan meant he could always make his way there. It did a number on me because every time I saw a specific car I had panic attacks so many times to the point I became a hermit and simply didn't want to leave the house. I suffered from extreme levels of PTSD and was sleepwalking; within the dream, I would see all the hurt and abuse I went through. Even to this day it's left a heavy mark on me as I am still taking therapy and my PTSD is a lot better now.

Losing a loved one too soon is an incredibly painful experience. It's natural to feel overwhelmed with grief, anger, and a range of other emotions. It's important to remember that there is no "right" way to grieve and that everyone experiences loss differently.

During this difficult time, it can be helpful to surround yourself with loved ones who can offer support and comfort. Sharing memories and stories about your loved one can also be a meaningful way to honor their memory and find solace in the good times you shared together.

It's important to take care of yourself during this time as well. Try to maintain healthy habits like eating well, getting enough sleep, and exercising regularly. Engaging in activities that you enjoy or finding ways to express your feelings through writing, art, or other forms of creative expression can also be helpful.

It's normal to feel a range of emotions after losing a loved one, including sadness, anger, guilt, and confusion.

Remember that there is no "right" way to feel and that it's okay to take the time you need to process your emotions.

As time passes, you may find that the intensity of your grief lessens, but it's important to remember that the loss will always be a part of your life. It's okay to continue to feel sadness or to remember your loved one with fondness and love.

If you find that you're struggling to cope with your grief, don't hesitate to reach out to a professional for help. Therapy, counseling, and support groups can all be helpful resources for processing your emotions and finding ways to move forward after a loss.

First Memory

My very first memory with my mother was at my great grandmothers' house. My mother had visiting rights and I went to visit where I saw my mother in an argument with my stepfather. They were constantly arguing and not stopping. I still remember it like it was yesterday, he grabbed my arm and shoved me into this dark room with plywood on the windows and I can hear the screams of my mother and the sounds of her being abused as she was being thrown around and all I can do was cry because I wasn't able to help her. After some time passed, I heard the door unlock after which when I opened it and heard my step-father drive off. I went to my mother and she was lying on the bed crying, her eyes were purple and I could see blood running down her nose and ears. I could not understand much and I brought her a towel. It was very confusing for me since I didn't understand what had happened. She was fine a few minutes ago and now her face is completely changed. My stepfather was abusive on and off and he didn't like the fact I was from my mothers' first marriage. He often would say crude and disgusting things to me like *"You should call me daddy because I pay for your mom to live"* or something like *"Without me and my money your mom would be out on the streets"*.

Chapter 5: Walking Away

"This chapter is going to be about my life when I walked away from my old family and to my new one. I will be comparing and contrasting my own family with my husband's family and also talking about his journey towards achieving his dreams"

Walking away from your toxic family can be one of the most difficult decisions a person can make. Our families are supposed to be the people who love us unconditionally, support us through thick and thin, and be there for us whenever we need them. Unfortunately, not all families are healthy, and some may even be toxic to our mental and emotional well-being. In this chapter, we will discuss the reasons why people may choose to walk away from their toxic families, the challenges they may face in doing so, and the steps they can take to heal and move forward.

Toxic family members can take many forms, from emotionally abusive parents to controlling siblings or extended family members. These toxic individuals may manipulate, gaslight, or belittle their loved ones, leaving them feeling powerless and helpless. They may also refuse to take responsibility for their actions, blaming their loved ones for their problems and refusing to acknowledge their own role in creating a toxic dynamic.

One of the main reasons why people choose to walk away from their toxic families is to protect their own mental and emotional health. Being constantly subjected to emotional abuse, manipulation, or control can take a toll on a person's self-esteem, leaving them feeling anxious, depressed, or even suicidal. Walking away from a toxic family can be a difficult decision, but it is often necessary to preserve one's own well-being.

Another reason why people may choose to walk away from their toxic families is to break the cycle of abuse. Many individuals who come from toxic families may find themselves repeating the same patterns of behavior as their parents or other family members. Walking away from a toxic family can give individuals the space they need to reflect on their own patterns of behavior and make a conscious effort to break the cycle of abuse.

Of course, walking away from a toxic family is not an easy decision to make. It can be emotionally wrenching to cut ties with the people who have been a part of your life for so long, even if they have been toxic. Many individuals who are considering walking away from their toxic families may struggle with feelings of guilt or shame, believing that they are somehow responsible for the toxic dynamic. They may also worry about how their decision will be perceived by others, or how it will impact their relationships with other family members.

Walking away from a toxic family can also be a challenging process. Individuals who have decided to cut ties with their toxic family members may need to create new support systems, such as therapy or support groups, to help them cope with the emotional fallout of their decision. They may also need to establish clear boundaries with other family members, or even cut ties with them if they are unwilling or unable to respect those boundaries. This can be a painful and difficult process, but it is often necessary for individuals to heal and move forward.

So, what steps can individuals take to heal and move forward after walking away from their toxic families? Here are a few suggestions:

1. Seek professional help: Walking away from a toxic family can be a traumatic experience. It's important to seek the help of a therapist or counselor who can help

you process your emotions and develop coping strategies.

2. Build a support system: It's important to surround yourself with people who love and support you. This may include friends, family members who are not toxic, or members of a support group.

3. Set boundaries: It's important to establish clear boundaries with family members who are toxic, and to stick to them. This may mean limiting contact, refusing to engage in toxic behavior, or even cutting ties altogether.

4. Practice self-care: It's important to take care of yourself physically, emotionally, and mentally. This may mean getting enough sleep, exercising regularly, eating a healthy diet, and engaging in activities that bring you joy.

Leaving behind my old family and embracing my new one was one of the most challenging decisions I have ever had to make. The journey was tough and emotionally draining, but it was also the most rewarding experience of my life. It all started when I realized that my old family was not providing me with the support and love that I needed. I knew that I had to make a change if I wanted to find true happiness and fulfillment.

I tried to make things work for a long time, but it became clear that I needed to break free from the negative energy and toxicity that surrounded me. I decided to take the leap and walk away from my old family to start a new life.

It was a difficult decision to make, and it took me a while to come to terms with the fact that I would be leaving behind everything I had ever known. However, I knew that I needed to do this for myself and my own mental health.

The first few months were tough. I felt alone and isolated, and I struggled to find my place in the world. However, I soon discovered that there were people out there who cared about me and wanted to support me. I found a new family in my husband's family and in the community that I had become a part of.

These new relationships were based on love, respect, and mutual support. I no longer felt like an outsider, and I finally had the space and freedom to pursue my dreams and passions.

It wasn't always easy, and there were times when I questioned my decision. However, I knew deep down that I had made the right choice. I was finally able to be myself and live my life on my own terms.

One of the most significant benefits of walking away from my old family was that I was able to heal from the wounds of the past. I was no longer living in a toxic environment, and I had the freedom to process my emotions and work through my trauma.

It wasn't always a smooth journey, and there were times when I struggled with feelings of guilt and shame. However, I soon realized that these emotions were a natural part of the process, and that it was okay to feel them.

As time went on, I grew stronger and more confident. I realized that I was capable of achieving my goals and that I had the support of an entire community behind me.

Today, I am grateful for the decision I made to leave my old family and start a new life. It was a difficult journey, but it was also the most rewarding experience of my life.

I learned that family is not just about blood ties, but about the people who love and support you unconditionally. I am now surrounded by people who accept me for who I am and who encourage me to be the best version of myself.

Leaving my old family was a difficult decision, but it was also the best decision I ever made. It allowed me to break free from the negativity and toxicity of the past and start a new life filled with love, support, and happiness.

You need to take charge of your life when you're dealing with a dysfunctional family. You need to start planning for the future if you want to get out of a toxic relationship. You can't sit back and expect things to improve on their own.

It is never simple to leave a dysfunctional, toxic family environment. However, you can begin making changes once you know what you want. As the first step toward recovery from abusive environments, you must begin to prioritize your own needs over those of your family.

We can do amazing things in our own lives when we are able to harness our own power without the assistance of harmful relatives. In order to assist you in devising an escape strategy, you ought to talk to a trusted friend or family member.

Above all else, you should try not to feel bad about leaving a dysfunctional family because you almost always gave your family plenty of chances to change their harmful ways. This is your chance to stand tall and pursue your own happiness without being constrained by others.

After moving to North Carolina, I started to experience what life was like in a stable household where no one is screaming at each other where everyone is supportive of each other, not judging one another or having bad blood. It made me so angry knowing how life can be so good and there was the envy of sorts knowing I could have grown up in a better home. It was the polar opposite to the life I had lived with Viky, who was loud and abusive. Compare that to my husband's stepfather and mother who were soft spoken, intelligent and kind people who are true Christians. My husband's stepfather was in the military. His biological father was in the picture when he was younger until he found a new wife who had two autistic sons which led him to not really having a relationship with my husband. He also never acknowledged my husband's achievements and always made light of the advances in life that my husband worked so hard to obtain, so it's better this way.

There was a clear contrast in even family meals where my family had a real disconnect with each other while on the other hand my in-laws weren't disconnected because they are a Christian family so they prayed every chance they got. Even when sitting down for meals they would pray first. Another part that still baffles me is the fact that we live in such a big house, especially compared to the one I used to where it looked like a creaking shack (The home I lived in back in Texas had floor boards so warped that the floor had a dip in the center of the living room from all the activity in that room). Even the fact that I got my own room was just unbelievable, considering I was sharing my room as a kid with my aunt or dad (whoever was living at home at the time).

My husband truly was blessed that he had a great family that supported him. His paternal aunt and her husband, his uncle, were like mentors to him and his uncle was like a father figure when he didn't have a father to go to. He got him to start cooking and inspired him to become a chef. So, when he lost his uncle to a severe stroke it was something that devastated him. He felt as if he had lost his actual father.

Moving forward his sister is amazing and has great kids a person can ask for. Her husband is also in the army and both I and my husband are inspired by their family dynamics. Their oldest son who is 11 years old is so smart as he is reading at 10th grade level. The intelligence that has been taught and instilled into my sister in laws children is amazing. She has a master's degree in Childhood Education and it shows through her amazing and intelligent children.

His best friend and his best friend's wife are very close to him. My husband arrived in Texas in 2009 with his family, as their new stationing through the army, and when he met them, they just hit it off. His best friend really helped him get structure to his life through high school all the way through to after the death of his uncle. He was supportive as he also helped my husband lose weight back when he was in high school. They went to college together and that's how I met my husband. We met at Texas A & M University – Kingsville, Tx Campus as he was going to college, for civil engineering but changed his mind to becoming a chef, and I was going to college for Deictics with a minor in Spanish (we didn't graduate due to unforeseen circumstances with finances and family issues). Anyway, I had to pass his best friend's test of trust before my husband decided to make it official with me but luckily when I first met his best friend and his wife (a beautiful, well-mannered, calm-tempered, and extremely intelligent woman) we hit it off right away! We had a lot of fun together and they showed me how fun people could be, again.

Even though I was angry, I still missed my family - which is a strange feeling. I guess you can never choose your family no matter what you do. I missed Lupe and my paternal uncle the most and even though my paternal uncle sided with my grandmother the most, even when she kicked me and my husband out of the house, I still couldn't help but miss him. My uncle told me to stay and submit to the wits and will of my paternal grandmother but it was a trap, a trap I had been living all my life. I knew that if I stayed, I would never escape and continue to feel like I was a caged animal. Viky always told me that I "owed" her my life because she *"saved me"* from my mother and stepfather.

My husband, whom I love and adore with all my heart, wanted to join the military and knew that it was going to be a difficult life but wanted to do it because he wanted to provide for us and was ready to make the sacrifice but as fate would have it he was diagnosed with a rare medical condition, called Rhabdomyolysis, which led him not making the cut. This was difficult since we knew we had to find a way to survive, and this is where my husband's passion for cooking came in. My husband always wanted to be a chef and this was the motivation he needed to live his dream. It all started with my husband working at Ihop as a dish washer to other franchise restaurants like Chili's as a line cook , McDonalds as a Manager, and whatnot. It was when he was working at chili's that he was suggested by his General Manager to go to a five-star restaurant, where he went to, and I joined him later as I was working at a different job already. After I left my previous job, we were working at the five-star restaurant that the General Manager referred my husband to, which is a Italian restaurant with French techniques. The chef, and owner, is highly trained, and also a former professor from a culinary school, he taught us both everything as he was a master chef (We answer to him as "Yes, Chef"). My husband and I really became really one with each other at this job. We both took interests in different ways with the job. My husband slowly made his way up the ladder of responsibility at the five-star restaurant. Chef has two more restaurants; one is a more laid-back place and we also work there – the second is in Belize and is currently in the works to be completed and we hope to have the chance to go to Belize for the culinary experience and knowledge. Chef is very successful and we look up to him very much. We one day hope to own and operate the five-star restaurant as partners with Chef or the other chefs we work with.

Also, let's not forget the delights/perks I get for being married to a chef! My husband makes the best food for me like he makes the best grits in town. These grits are so velvety, rich, buttery, and savory all at once – not too salty, not under-seasoned - what he makes represents who he is. He makes amazing mac and cheese which is seven-layered, he makes garlic mashed potatoes, and also, he makes an amazing pan-seared fried chicken which is an umami of flavor in your mouth. I love when he cooks me a medium-rare steak with broccolini and fingerling potatoes. Lastly, though the thing I loved most that he made was fish, it was truly divine. The flaky pieces attached to the crispy and crunchy skin at the bottom is always the best food I can ask from my husband.

We both love food (and to eat it!) so cooking felt safe and comfortable with us. Plus, we always felt like food is what brings people together and that's what we wanted for our future – togetherness, happiness, and a family of our own one day. We both feel like the word "family" is misrepresented in this time and age. Family is the people who are there for you no matter what – literally give you the shirt off of their back for you even if it meant that they (themselves) would not have an extra shirt – THAT is family. Someone who is willing to answer that call at 3am – 4am because you can't sleep or for whatever reason is family.

One of the things that I had time to think about was why people acted the way they acted, like my paternal grandmother, and my stepfather who treated me like a burden. One of the things that people are now discovering is something called generational trauma.

Generational trauma is a term that refers to the

passing down of traumatic experiences and their effects from one generation to the next. This can include psychological and emotional trauma resulting from events such as war, genocide, slavery, and other forms of oppression. The concept of generational trauma recognizes that traumatic experiences can have a lasting impact on individuals and communities and that these effects can be transmitted across generations.

One of the key characteristics of generational trauma is that it can be both explicit and implicit. Explicit forms of generational trauma can include the transmission of traumatic memories, stories, and experiences from one generation to the next. This can involve parents or grandparents sharing their own experiences of trauma, or it can involve cultural traditions or rituals that commemorate traumatic events. Implicit forms of generational trauma are more subtle and can include the transmission of attitudes, beliefs, and behaviors that are shaped by traumatic experiences.

One way that generational trauma can manifest itself is through patterns of behavior and coping mechanisms that are passed down from one generation to the next. For example, a child of an alcoholic parent may grow up to have their own issues with substance abuse, or the child of a parent who experienced domestic violence may struggle with trust and intimacy in their own relationships. These patterns can become ingrained in families and communities over time, leading to a cycle of trauma and dysfunction that can be difficult to break.

Another way that generational trauma can impact individuals and communities is through the transmission of stress and anxiety. Trauma can leave individuals with a heightened sense of stress and a reduced ability to cope with difficult situations. This stress can be transmitted across generations, leading to higher rates of mental health issues, such as anxiety, depression, and post-traumatic stress disorder (PTSD). This can also have a broader impact on communities, with higher rates of poverty, crime, and substance abuse being associated with generational trauma.

One of the challenges of addressing generational trauma is that it can be difficult to identify and acknowledge. Trauma is often stigmatized and can be seen as a personal failing or weakness, rather than a result of external circumstances. This can make it difficult for individuals and communities to acknowledge the impact that trauma has had on their lives and to seek the help and support they need to heal.

However, there are a range of approaches that can be used to address generational trauma. One of the most important is to create safe and supportive environments where individuals and communities can share their experiences and stories. This can involve creating support groups, offering counseling and therapy services, and providing education and training on trauma-informed care. It can also involve developing cultural and community-specific approaches to healing, such as traditional healing practices, storytelling, and art therapy.

Another important approach is to address the root causes of trauma, such as poverty, inequality, and discrimination. This can involve working to reduce systemic barriers and create more equitable opportunities for individuals and communities. It can also involve addressing historical injustices and acknowledging the impact that past traumas have had on different groups.

Ultimately, addressing generational trauma requires a multifaceted approach that recognizes the complex and interconnected nature of trauma and its effects. It requires a commitment to creating safe and supportive environments, to addressing the root causes of trauma, and to promoting healing and resilience across generations. By doing so, we can help individuals and communities break the cycle of trauma and move towards a more hopeful and healthy future.

Chapter 6: "Forgotten"

"This chapter is where I talk about how my trauma affected everything around me along with the struggles that followed"

Trauma can have a profound and lasting impact on an individual's life, affecting not only their own well-being but also those around them. This chapter will explore the ways in which trauma can ripple through an individual's life, leaving a trail of struggles and challenges in its wake.

My own experience of trauma began when I was just a child. Growing up in a household where abuse and neglect were common, I quickly learned that the world was not a safe or predictable place. I became hypervigilant and anxious, constantly on edge and anticipating the next outburst of violence or neglect.

As I grew older, the impact of my trauma began to manifest in a variety of ways. I struggled with depression and anxiety, as well as physical symptoms such as chronic pain and digestive issues. This led to eating disorders and my weight fluctuating rapidly up and down on the scale. My relationships with others were fraught with difficulty, as I struggled to trust and connect with others. Many of my peers thought of me as an intense and strange person. I was "all over the place" with my emotions and how I behaved when I wasn't at home. I tried my best to fit in and make friends as best as I could but once we became adults a lot of us went our separate ways.

One of the most profound ways in which my trauma affected those around me was in my interactions with my family. Despite the fact that my paternal grandmother was one of the sources of my trauma, I found myself drawn back to them time and time again, seeking their approval and validation. This resulted in a pattern of unhealthy and co-dependent relationships that further exacerbated my struggles with mental health.

My trauma also affected my ability to form healthy and stable relationships with others. I found myself drawn to individuals who mirrored the unhealthy dynamics of my childhood, seeking out partners who were emotionally unavailable or abusive. This led to a cycle of repeated trauma, as I found myself once again in situations where I felt powerless and unsafe.

Perhaps one of the most challenging aspects of dealing with trauma is the way in which it can permeate every aspect of one's life. From work to friendships to hobbies, my trauma was always there, lurking beneath the surface and threatening to derail any progress I had made.

At work, I struggled with feelings of inadequacy and self-doubt, constantly worrying that I was not good enough and that I would be exposed as a fraud. This led to a cycle of overwork and burnout, as I pushed myself to prove my worth and avoid the shame and humiliation of failure.

In my social life, I found it difficult to connect with others and form lasting relationships. I often felt like an outsider, unable to relate to others and lacking the social skills necessary to form meaningful connections.

Even my hobbies and interests were not immune from the effects of my trauma. I found myself avoiding activities that I once enjoyed, as they reminded me of a time before my trauma when life felt simpler and more manageable.

Overall, my experience with trauma has been one of ongoing struggle and challenge. Despite the many obstacles I have faced, however, I have also found moments of strength and resilience. Through therapy and support from loved ones, I have begun to reclaim my life and move forward in a positive direction.

While trauma can have a profound and lasting impact on an individual's life, it is also important to remember that healing and growth are possible. With the right resources and support, it is possible to overcome the struggles that follow trauma and reclaim one's life.

Tragedy is invisible to many of us, we hide from it, run from it if we can because it feels so distant and far away. It's only when it's at our door step that we truly believe it exists. It's hard knowing that you exist with all this pain. The tragedy of my life was growing up with people who were controlling, judging, and uncaring. Carrying this entire trauma led me to carry all the demons of the past with me.

I was at work when I lost my temper with someone who was messing around with me and I completely lost it when I started screaming and abusing that person. It was then I decided to go to a professional who diagnosed me with C-PTSD. They told me that because of my childhood and past traumas I had been suffering from C-PTSD which is also the reason I was drinking constantly and not taking care of myself. I drank to forget my past and not deal with the issue head-on. I was waking up craving that poison constantly; shaking from withdrawal and anxiety I constantly felt like "I HAD TO HAVE IT". I couldn't function at my job without having some sort of "buzz".

I was lost in the grips of my alcoholism and was drowning from the inside out. I developed G.E.R.D. (gastroesophageal reflux disease) from drinking so much liquor because it was available to me at serval of the restaurants I used to work at so it felt like easy pickings for me. Almost like I was a little kid in a candy store; I had every kind of alcohol I could ask for and more, plus, my co-workers, who were bartenders, unknowingly was helping fuel the fire of my addiction and that's what was so hard about being around my addiction constantly.

Not many individuals get away from some type of injury in their lives. The majority of people survive personal tragedies by developing physical or emotional escape plans that help them deal with the situation at the time.

The development of an emotional wall that aids in separating the individual from the incident is one of the most prevalent of these defensive strategies. It is a secretive haven where he or she can somehow manage their agony, which they or cannot leave.

The majority of people, whether they are aware of it or not, carry these havens of escape into intimate relationships in adulthood. They are oblivious default reactions that are at any point prepared to keep away from the aggravation of possibly reappearing past injuries. When activated, they let a person hide behind the walls that are still there, keeping them captive to their past pain and preventing them from being fully present in the relationship they are in now. Relationships are hard to maintain and feel like you are questioning their every word, sentence, motive, or action because you have a sense of untrust wrapped in fear from the past traumas and negative experiences.

There are numerous manifestations of these emotional walls. They can be subtle and slow to appear at times, or they can be intense and reactive, appearing out of nowhere. It's possible that the partner who hides behind those walls of protection does not even realize that they are still dealing with the pain of the initial trauma.

A person who is experiencing a trigger for a previous traumatic event is experiencing the same agony as if it were happening again right now. Any behavior that brings back memories of the previous traumatic event can set it off.

The partner who is going through these intense feelings again might suddenly snap, walk away, attack back, or become immobile and unable to do anything. It is evident that they are responding to their partner as if they were a person from the past. Their feelings are out of control, and they act as if they are about to die, retreating into their once-safe haven right away.

There is a possibility that the partners who are reliving their trauma will break apart if they are unable to construct their walls sufficiently quickly. They frequently decompensate by exhibiting pain, rage, confusion, or helplessness when they are made vulnerable and exposed in this manner. They cannot control the torrent of emotions that come over them like a bursting dam, seemingly out of nowhere. As a result of prolonged suppression that they are unable to bear, meltdowns frequently accurately qualify as a PTSD response. Partners on the other end, who may or may not be aware of the previous trauma, frequently feel helpless and unsure of what to do. The partner may experience feelings of abandonment as a result of their own need to retreat as a result of those feelings of powerlessness. If that ends up being a repeat of the initial trauma, their need to disconnect immediately becomes even more pressing.

Partners who are on the other side of spontaneous and rapidly erupting walls frequently report that those partners appear to be someone else. Alcohol or drugs may also open the door to less inhibition, which makes it easy to blame the sudden outburst rather than the realization that the hidden trauma is the real problem.

At some point, those sudden outbursts and the personality shifts that frequently accompany them will emerge on their own. A person who is usually easygoing and compatible can suddenly explode in anger and blame, threaten to leave, make statements that will wipe out everything, or not be open to any kind of resolution.

Not all reactive behaviors involve rage. In an urgent need to physically distance themselves from the entangling circumstance they are in, some people may simply retreat into silence. They might convey that urgency with finality as if they are never going to return, which may make their partners panic and fearful.

I became extremely dependent on my husband because of my trauma; I latched on to him in a suffocating way. When I was drunk, I used to argue with my husband and became self-deprecating which my husband did not understand since at that point none of us knew what I was going through. It really did take a toll since I was not in control of my emotions and I did not understand how to cope with an understanding family. I could feel the waves of chaos reeling inside of me; chaos was something I was so accustomed to and to suddenly not have it apart of your life, strangely, left a void and I didn't understand how to fill that void. I felt like I had a tumor removed from my body the size of a bowling ball but was left gaping open and bleeding out. Here I am, left with is gaping hole, that wasn't a negative one but it was still a hole. Along with that hole I felt a lot of weight on my shoulders from leaving my family behind also. I had to figure out how I was going to live with the guilt of having to walk away and how I was going to "justify" myself to my loved ones. This pushed me further and further into my drinking which began to lead me into abusing my anxiety medications to even further numb myself. My husband was watching me be destructive and was doing his best to maintain our household and also up-hold his eccentric alcoholic wife.

He has always been supportive unlike my paternal grandmother who always questioned my husband, saying things like he tried to make a pass at my paternal-aunt and also say he was cheating on me, since he was doing odd jobs, three of them, at the time, to be exact – I knew he wasn't doing those things. She did not see him as a hard worker but instead a dead beat not to mention me being of Mexican decent and I married to a white man this led to them disowning me. They were extremely abusive towards my husband who was nothing but caring and compare that to when we were living with his parents who were overly supportive the difference is night and day.

Loss of hope is something I have dealt with throughout my life, and without hope life isn't worth living. Hope gives us something to live for and keeps us moving forward. Maintaining resilience in the face of difficulties and dealing with life's challenges require hope. Even a glimmer of hope that things will improve can motivate us.

However, things can appear hopeless when we begin to lose hope. We may begin to believe that there is nothing left to live for when we encounter constant resistance and are unable to achieve our objectives. What's the point of trying if we can't get to where we want to be and don't feel in charge of our lives?

Unexpected circumstances began to arise as we worked toward our objectives. We should have been prepared to manage hindrances and downsides, but we were so young we mishandled finances and many other things which led to my husband and I being homeless once and then almost a second time. We thought about the obstacles we might have encountered and how we could handle them. At the point when they emerged, we will be prepared, have an arrangement, and will not have the option to blame this so as to surrender. It will likewise be a significant guide to the progress of our objectives. The main component that helped our relationship continue was never blaming each other. We made sure to hold ourselves accountable for all of our short-comings, and then we would discuss what we needed to learn from our down-fall. The few things that have helped keep our relationship afloat are: accountability, honesty, and trust.

Talking about today though I am a completely different person. I am more hopeful through the love and support of my current family which is my husband's family and my mother's side of my family.

I wrote a letter to myself; it helped me cope.

"It was a difficult realization to come to, that the pain and trauma of your past had been affecting your life in such profound ways. But it was also a turning point, a moment of clarity that allowed you to see the root of your struggles and take action to heal. Seeking professional help and getting a diagnosis of C-PTSD was an important step in your journey towards recovery.

It wasn't easy, of course. Breaking free from addiction is a grueling and ongoing process, and it's especially difficult when you're surrounded by triggers and temptations. But you found the strength to face your demons head-on and take control of your life.

As you started to heal, you began to see the world in a different way. The tragedy that had always seemed so far away was suddenly all around you, and you realized how many people were carrying their own invisible pain. It gave you a new sense of empathy and understanding, and it inspired you to share your own story with others who might be struggling in silence.

Today, you're still on your journey towards recovery, but you've made incredible progress. You've learned to care for yourself in ways that were once unimaginable, and you've found a sense of purpose in helping others. The tragedy of your past will always be a part of you, but you've learned to carry it with grace and strength. And you've shown that it's possible to find hope and healing even in the darkest of places.

This journey hasn't been walking through the park but more like a stroll through the 9 circles of hell all the way down to Lucifer himself. The *Divine Comedy* by *Dante Alighieri* is a book that will open your eyes to how much you are really struggling. I wish you could have read this book when you needed it most, but better late than never. And, I hope one day you will gain the courage to write the book you have been always wanting to write."

Chapter 7: Memories and Nightmares

"It's hard leaving the past behind you. Just when you think you are free, it rears its ugly head. This chapter will go into how my past nightmares always is right behind me like a dark shadow"

When we are kids we are always afraid of the dark, I never really thought why that was the case with most children. Is it the unknown that scares us as kids and is it that we cannot see beyond the darkness, either way as adults we think we become braver but the reality is we exchange those fears for other ones. Fears that lead to our traumas.

Memories are often forgotten, but nightmares are never forgotten. They linger in the back of our minds, constantly reminding us of the terror we experienced. But what if our memories and nightmares could be used to our advantage? That's exactly what we can do – use both to our benefit. We can learn from our memories, understanding what works and what doesn't, allowing us to make better decisions in the present. We can use our nightmares to remind us of potential dangers and give us an idea of how to avoid them. By combining the two, we can create a powerful tool to better our lives. Memory and nightmares can teach us to be more aware of our surroundings and ourselves, and help us become more successful in whatever we decide to pursue. So don't be afraid of your memories or nightmares – use them as a tool for personal growth and success.

Do you ever feel like life is a never-ending cycle of memories and nightmares? Well, you're not alone! From the moment we wake up, our thoughts and feelings are constantly bombarded with the memories of yesterday, the hopes of tomorrow, and the nightmares of the things we'd rather forget. We may try to run away from our memories and nightmares, but they will always be there, chasing us through our days and nights. It's important to remember that these memories can both haunt and inspire us, depending on how we choose to channel them. So let's challenge ourselves to take a deep breath and look at our memories and nightmares with a sense of wit and humor. After all, life is too short to take ourselves too seriously.

Memories and nightmares are two sides of the same coin. Memories are beautiful and vivid, often serving as a source of joy, comfort, and nostalgia. Nightmares, on the other hand, can be terrifying and unsettling. While nightmares can be unpleasant and even traumatic experiences, understanding them and the feelings they evoke can be an important part of self-care. To start, it's important to recognize that nightmares are a common and normal occurrence. Everyone has nightmares from time to time, even if they don't usually remember them. It's also important to understand the different types of nightmares. Some might be triggered by real-life events while others are simply the product of a vivid imagination. In addition, nightmares can take many forms - from strange creatures to natural disasters - and come with a variety of feelings, such as fear and confusion. While some people may find relief in discussing their nightmares with friends or family members, seeking professional help can be beneficial for those who feel overwhelmed by them. Ultimately, it's important to remember that memories and nightmares are part of life and that understanding both can help us become more aware of our own emotions.

Memories are vital to our sense of identity and our ability to make sense of the world. They provide us with an important connection to our past, and can be a source of comfort, joy, and inspiration. At the same time, memories can also haunt us in the form of nightmares. Nightmares are an expression of powerful emotions that can leave a lasting impression on our minds, even if we can't always remember the details of the dream. It is important to understand the relationship between memories and nightmares, in order to process our emotions in a healthy way. Memories can often be a source of anxiety, fear, and sadness, which can manifest itself in the form of nightmares. When we are able to recognize and understand these connections between our memories and nightmares, we have an opportunity to process those emotions in a meaningful way. Doing so can help us find peace and closure after difficult experiences, or provide us with a better understanding of our past. By acknowledging these connections between memories and nightmares, we can begin to heal from our past and create a brighter future for ourselves.

There came a point in my life where I would have nightmares about my grandmother and I could see her everywhere I went. My husband would look at me standing in staring in to the distance completely lost. Even worse was when I used to see my mother. This was painful because once in a while you wake up and for a second forget your loved ones are not there anymore. There was also this person who resembled my mom, she used to say good morning to me every day. I used to work in a restaurant with her and I told her everything about my mom after which she hugged me tightly so leaving that job was hard.

Moving forward I had terrible nightmares as I would wake up sweating or screaming, even having sleep paralysis where I couldn't move. The nights were long, dark and full of terror as I had to deal with these issues constantly. I was at war with myself, I would cry or have panic attacks.

It can be unsettling to wake up with vivid nightmare memories or vivid dreams. Although there hasn't been much research on the hypothesis that nightmares can cause trauma, the answer to this question may depend on how trauma is defined.

Over time, definitions of what constitutes trauma have evolved. Psychologists used the term "trauma" to describe events that were outside of the normal range of human experiences because, in the beginning, it was believed that trauma could only occur while a person was awake. The term "trauma" has been defined more broadly over time, taking into account the many different types of traumatic experiences and their effects over time.

The body's fight-flight-freeze response is activated in response to a frightening event in order to safeguard us. As the body releases stress hormones, our pupils dilate, and our heart rate rises, we become hypersensitive to danger. This alarm system typically quiets down and resumes normal operation after we have had time to process a traumatic event.

Knowing when to ask for help is an essential part of dealing with traumatic experiences. Traumatic events and their repercussions can be treated by medical professionals, counselors, and therapists.

Having bad dreams and trouble resting are ordinary encounters after emergencies and injury and many individuals recuperate from injury-related dreams without treatment. Some people may be concerned that these problems could lead to a more serious condition like post-traumatic stress disorder (PTSD).

Ten years had passed since the death of my mother, and it always felt like it was yesterday. The longing just doesn't ever go away, especially for the people on my mother's side who I had spent a year with. Those were the people I was supposed to be with. My maternal grandmother supported me in each and every way. She was supportive of what I wanted to do with my life, which was the kind of support I always needed but didn't have. Those ten years have been tough since I was looking after my mental health, I was told at the age of 25 that my liver was 20 percent damaged and I was essentially killing myself, and had to stop. From then on, I went cold turkey and stopped what I was doing. I stopped smoking and drinking and started to follow a straight and narrow path. The years of partying didn't do me any good as I was trying to push the negative thoughts in my head to the back of my mind.

The day came when my paternal grandmother passed away. My entire paternal family mourned her as they had lost the matriarch in their family but for me it was a weight lifted off my shoulders. Now I know that might sound cruel but it is not that at all. I didn't want her to die or wished ill harm to her in any way I simply felt her shadow behind me. She was one of the main culprits for my abuse, and was she defended by my other relatives when she used to abuse me. My uncle told me she was disciplining me and that it was for my own good but in saying that, I truly do forgive her, even though she has done me wrong and she never apologized once in her life.

Can a person who has passed away be forgiven? The wounds of the past may still be very much present in those who have been left behind, even though the other person is no longer among the living. It seems natural to try to take the best medicine to get rid of resentment when it persists in you. Despite the fact that forgiveness is such potent medicine, the deceased individual cannot now demonstrate remorse, repent, or make amends in any way. In the living world, reconciliation is no longer possible. It's possible that it's now impossible to forgive someone who has passed away. Let's look at this situation from five different angles to see if we can answer the question.

A moral virtue comparable to justice, patience, and kindness is the capacity to forgive. Understanding and displaying each virtue requires varying degrees of perfection. Perfection in the context of forgiveness entails: a) Recognize that you were wronged; b) Be prepared to let go of resentment and take steps to lessen it; and c) unconditionally love the person who treated you unfairly. In addition, when the other person readily accepts the offer of forgiveness, becomes trustworthy, and the two or more people have a genuine reconciliation that brings them back together with respect, trust, and love, the interpersonal perfection of the forgiveness is reached.

Any moral virtue can be practiced even if one does not achieve perfection in it. In the case of forgiveness, the virtue is still exercised even if the forgiver shows restraint in seeking vengeance and is respectful without feeling loved or having the will to love. Even though it is imperfect, it is still forgiveness. If there is a willingness to reconcile, even if it may never happen, the one who was offended is still practicing the moral virtue of forgiveness, even if what I refer to as interpersonal perfection is not achieved. The eagerness frequently is brought to a genuine compromise provided that different changes and isn't a danger to the forgiver.

Forgiveness is a moral virtue that involves releasing feelings of anger, resentment, or revenge towards someone who has wronged us. It is an act of mercy and compassion that allows us to move forward from a hurtful experience, while also freeing the offender from guilt and shame. Forgiveness is often associated with interpersonal perfection, but it is important to note that forgiveness can still be practiced imperfectly.

The act of forgiving requires restraint in seeking vengeance and respecting the offender without necessarily feeling love or having the will to love. This can be challenging, especially if the wrongdoing was significant and caused a great deal of pain. However, even if the forgiver is not able to completely let go of their negative emotions, simply choosing to refrain from seeking revenge is an act of forgiveness in itself.

Furthermore, forgiveness does not necessarily

require a willingness to reconcile with the offender. While reconciliation is often seen as the ultimate goal of forgiveness, it is not always possible or even advisable. In cases where the offender is unrepentant or the relationship is toxic, reconciliation may not be a safe or healthy option. In such cases, practicing forgiveness can still be beneficial for the forgiver, as it allows them to let go of negative emotions and move on with their lives.

It is also important to note that forgiveness is not a one-time event, but rather a process that takes time and effort. Even if the forgiver is able to forgive initially, it is possible for negative emotions to resurface later on, especially if they are triggered by a similar situation or behavior. In such cases, it is important for the forgiver to continue practicing forgiveness and to seek support from others if needed.

While forgiveness is a moral virtue that can be practiced imperfectly, it is important to note that there are some limitations to forgiveness. Forgiveness does not mean that the forgiver must forget the wrongdoing or excuse the offender's behavior. It also does not require the forgiver to continue to have a relationship with the offender, especially if doing so would be detrimental to their well-being.

In some cases, forgiveness may not be appropriate or even possible. For example, if the wrongdoing was particularly heinous, such as in cases of abuse or violence, forgiveness may not be possible or advisable. In such cases, it may be more appropriate for the victim to seek justice through legal means or to seek help from a therapist or support group.

In conclusion, forgiveness is a moral virtue that can be practiced imperfectly. Even if the forgiver is not able to completely let go of their negative emotions or is not willing to reconcile with the offender, simply choosing to refrain from seeking revenge is an act of forgiveness in itself. Forgiveness is a process that takes time and effort, and it is important to note that there are some limitations to forgiveness. However, when practiced appropriately, forgiveness can bring healing and freedom to both the forgiver and the offender.

Forgiveness does not require perfection on our part. Isn't it the same when learning to play sports or math? Even though she does not yet understand the more advanced mathematics of calculus, an adolescent who is just beginning to learn algebra is engaging in mathematical calculation. Even though he or she does not possess the skill of a professional soccer player, an adolescent still plays the sport.

It is not necessary to be able to express the virtue of appropriate forgiveness in its perfect essence of loving the other person or to be able to openly reconcile.

After my paternal grandmother's death and forgiving her I felt a weight lifted I could finally be myself and let go of the terrible traumas I had been through. It's a sense of freedom I had never felt before, I think the most important thing for me is to let go. I guess that is the most important lesson I had learned.

Chapter 8: Where is Home?

The age-old question of 'where is home?' has been pondered by many throughout the ages. Is home where you grew up? Is it the place you currently reside? Is it the place your heart yearns to be? Who knows! But one thing is for certain, home is a feeling, and it can be found in the most unlikely of places. Whether you're a nomad, traveler, or stay-at-home parent, we all have a place we call home. That place might be in the mountains, by a lake, or in a tiny apartment in the city. It could even be on a beach or deep in the jungle. Home is where you make it, so make sure it's somewhere you want to be! And don't forget to laugh along the way - that's what makes it home sweet home.

Where is home these days? It seems like a question that never has a clear answer. In a world that is constantly changing, it can be difficult to find a place you can call your own. The idea of home has become increasingly elusive, with people having to relocate for work, family, or personal reasons. We may have places we go to and people we love, but it's hard to find the same sense of security and comfort that we once had when we were younger. It's disheartening to know that we may never be able to find a place to settle permanently. We may never be able to come back to a place that was once our home. Even when we do, it often feels different from what it used to be. Home is something that changes over time, and it can be difficult to keep up with its ever-evolving nature. It's important for us to remember that home is not just a physical place; it's also the people we are surrounded by and the moments we share with them. Home is not just about where you live, but who you live with and how you live your life.

At this point in my life, I was going through a lot, mainly depression and anxiety, trying to fight off my demons. Depression is painful. Majorly. Feelings of low self-worth are one of the symptoms that can undermine confidence. When you're in the midst of a depressive episode, interactions that used to feel natural and easy can become overwhelming and frightening. I was in this constant battle with my mind and my heart. The war that was inside of me left me feeling like I had no one to trust, not even my husband, I felt like everyone had bad intentions towards me and wasn't going to allow me to "relax". Finding people, I could "relax" around was not something I came by often and when I wasn't around someone in my inner circle, I would feel like an animal cornered and needing to attack! I couldn't and wouldn't let my guard down around co-workers, my in-laws, or other relatives.

A fear of intimacy can last as long as the underlying root cause is present, just like depression itself. Getting help from a mental health professional can help you get better faster and stop running away from people. It can also be scary if you've developed a pattern of avoiding communication. Opening up can seem like a huge step if you're doing this because of a past trauma. However, don't worry. Slow and steady is best, just like in the previous step.

Consider how much vulnerability is necessary to maintain a relationship critically. It's possible that you don't have to immediately disclose your life story and all of the reasons why you struggle with intimacy. In fact, if the other person didn't know it was coming, that could make them overworked. Varying how much information you give out in each conversation can be a good way to keep people from being "put-off". That gives people time to consider the reasons behind your emotions. Additionally, it gives you time to comprehend their reaction without feeling overly vulnerable.

Although having these important conversations can be intimidating, it is highly likely that they will become easier over time, it's possible that communication is more of a sign than a foundation for healthy relationships.

Do you remember the first time you rode a bicycle? How did you have to consider each step, like keeping your balance and pointing with your hands? Now, when you ride a bike, you don't have to do that despite the difficulty, treat communication as a means to an end rather than an end in and of itself, despite the difficulty.

My husband and I were moving around a lot changing jobs and places which made wherever we went not feel like home. No matter where we went, I was not happy where I was and even in thinking of my hometown, that also did not feel like home even though that is why and changing. I was having a hard time coping with all the moving around and changing jobs, so it stirred up some issues with change and feeling like I didn't belong anywhere. I felt a lot of pressure of keeping jobs, maintaining my relationship, and then dealing with my mental health with no medication. These things were hard in itself and made the anxiety and depression deeper and deeper.

I learned during my mid-twenties that building a home wasn't the same as "making one". When we build, there is SO MUCH SUPPORT behind one another, but when we MAKE a home its often times forced or due to certain circumstances. Many people don't have the option to build a home, but only to make one realizing that it is all mirrors in rooms we are all passing through fading in and out of reality only surfacing when someone can snap you out of you haze.

In this point I wanted to talk about how we all are on the same earth just on different life paths. There are mirrors we are staring into saying "why me, why me", when there is someone else on the other side of that mirror simply smiling with tears and trying to hold I together for themselves, their family, or a loved one. These mirrors tie us all metaphorically to the same kind of pain and suffering. We are all standing in the same room staring at a mirror, oblivious to each other and I think it's time we start looking over to see if the person next to you just needs a helping hand or a reason to look away from that mirror and brighten their day so when they look back at the mirror there isn't so much pain and suffering left.

It's important to self-love, I believe no matter how hard it is. Simply put, loving yourself means treating yourself with the same care and respect as a friend or family member would. It indicates that you put in the effort to understand, value, and cultivate a relationship with yourself. In addition, it indicates that you will take care of yourself and develop habits that will both benefit your health and keep you safe.

"Love is patient and love is kind," as the saying goes. When you say you love yourself, you mean that you do the same for yourself as you would for other people. It encompasses everything you do for a loved one, such as recognizing your strengths and weaknesses, exchanging forgiveness with them, and so on.

When I'm in such a dark place, getting through the day takes a lot of time and effort. This unavoidable, highly self-critical, cyclical, and hateful inner dialogue is what I hear. It prevents me from experiencing any form of self-pity, from having healthy interactions with the people in my life, from engaging in any kind of motivated or productive work, even something as simple as emptying the trash, and, most of the time, even from getting enough sleep. A cement block can pile up on me day in and day out. It wears me down, makes me feel unvaluable, and it makes me feel ashamed, until I have no energy left to respond. The cement then trickles down to the rest of my body like a thick landslide that's holding me down in place with no escape.

During my darkest hours, I have discovered a few fairly dependable methods for giving myself a significant dose of self-love. Even though it's nice when people in my life offer words of support, nothing compares to loving oneself. It is extremely rewarding and helpful when I am able to find the time and energy to sit down and confront those negative thoughts. Meditation has become a dear friend of mine. Meditation allows me to calm my mind and soul from the chaos in my mind and around me. Sometimes the silence quiets the screams in my head but sometimes it makes them stronger. Even though, it can sometimes create an echo in my mind I know that those of cries of healing and not of distain.

I look in the mirror at myself. I give myself full attention and give myself praise, even if it seems forced or difficult. I cherish, love, and keep in mind that this is who I am right now, regardless of my future objectives, and in order to be a vehicle for change in my own life, I must accept and love who I am! However, I have created affirmations for myself on days when I need some passive self-love because it is not always easy to push through those negative thoughts and sometimes I do not have the energy.

We all make mistakes, give in when we shouldn't, and occasionally place the wrong priorities. Loving yourself and not beating yourself up means allowing yourself to make mistakes. When you focus on the things, you're not doing well with rather than the things you're doing well, you fall victim to the ugly and persistent negativity bias.

Another process is learning self-compassion, which involves accepting that you will make mistakes and that you are doing your best at the moment. It can make a big difference to acknowledge that to yourself and occasionally, if you're in hot water, to someone else. Accept that you will work to improve and that you have made a mistake. If you are picking up on a theme of acceptance here, well then you got it... because, that's kind of what we can do sometimes, and that is also fine. The key to success is acceptance.

I guess home is where the heart is and more importantly where you feel peace, and inner peace is the most important aspect of life, which I finally have.

Home is not a physical destination; it is a feeling.

Home is a place of comfort and security, a place where we can be ourselves and be surrounded by unconditional love.

Home is the place we come when we are tired, weary, and in need of a hug.

Home is the place we can always find acceptance, understanding, and support.

Home is the place where our heart can be filled with joy and contentment.

Everyone has their own definition of home and it looks different for each of us. It might be a place, a person, or an activity. Home is wherever you find peace, comfort, support, and happiness. Home can be any place as long as it is somewhere that brings you joy and happiness. Home is where you find yourself surrounded by love and acceptance. Wherever home may be for you, cherish it and embrace it for it is yours and yours alone to enjoy.

Chapter 9: "I can Do This"

"Redemption isn't easy to attain maybe that is why many people don't achieve it, thankfully I am the few lucky ones that do, and this is what the chapter is all about"

We all have demons—parts of ourselves that we don't like to admit but that we can see lurking within us. These demons cause us to act irrationally and selfishly rather than out of love or fear for ourselves.

However, despite our best efforts to ignore them, our demons are always present, rising to the surface and spilling out of the lid we try to put on them. And the more we try to keep that lid on, the worse things get in our lives. To forget our demons, we get high or drunk. Work or competition serve as distractions from our demons. We deceive ourselves into thinking that other people will eventually treat us like crap by treating them like crap.

Anything to keep the demons at bay... At some point, you've probably fought your demons: you've fought back feelings of anger or guilt, and you've hated yourself for your stupid actions. You've promised yourself that you'll either put the vodka away or stop listening to that inner voice.

My struggle with my own "usefulness" in this world frequently spirals to a dark and lonely place if I am not careful, even though we are all lazy slobs at least occasionally.

I tend to judge myself quite harshly when I procrastinate, telling myself that I'm a bad, lazy sack of shit. My general assumption is that everyone, with the exception of me, is productive and active every day. After many years, I now realize how irrational this belief is. Still, a small voice in my head tells me that no one else struggles to stay motivated, so I must be a loser.

Demons begin as self-criticism: You are unlovable, lazy, filthy, stupid, unlovable, etc.

Then, we make every effort to avoid that judgment and disprove it. Six times, we clean the garage. We put in 11 hours a day. At the local rink, we take home the blue ribbon. See! I told you I was cool and popular! See! I'm there!

However, this avoidance eventually becomes destructive to oneself. You clean the garage once more rather than picking up your children from school. You work so hard you fall asleep on the way home. Your partner will leave you yelling, "You never wanted me! " as a result of your obsession with skating rink blue ribbons. You simply desired someone to observe you skate!

Worse yet, despite your efforts to disprove your demon, it persists. The demon of laziness never ceases to make me feel lazy. For myself, I spent a lot of time partying to distract myself. Alcohol and pills, mostly.

Dealing with past demons is not an easy task, and it often requires a lot of courage, resilience, and support from others. Past demons can come in different forms, such as traumatic experiences, mistakes, regrets, or unresolved issues that continue to haunt us and affect our lives in negative ways. However, it is possible to overcome past demons and find peace and healing, and in this essay, we will explore some strategies that can help.

Acknowledge and Accept the Past.

The first step in dealing with past demons is to acknowledge and accept them. This means being honest with ourselves about what happened, how it affected us, and the role we played in it. It also means letting go of any denial, blame, or shame that may be preventing us from facing the truth. Acknowledging and accepting the past is not easy, but it is necessary for healing and growth.

Seek Professional Help.

Dealing with past demons can be overwhelming, and sometimes we need professional help to navigate through it. Therapists, counselors, or other mental health professionals can provide a safe and supportive environment where we can explore our emotions, thoughts, and behaviors related to the past. They can also teach us coping skills, relaxation techniques, and strategies for managing triggers and flashbacks.

Connect with Others.

Dealing with past demons can be isolating, and it is important to connect with others who can provide support, understanding, and empathy. This can be family, friends, support groups, or online communities that share similar experiences. Connecting with others can also provide a sense of validation, empowerment, and hope.

Practice Self-Care.

Dealing with past demons can be exhausting, and it is important to prioritize self-care to prevent burnout and promote healing. This can include regular exercise, healthy eating, getting enough sleep, practicing mindfulness, and engaging in hobbies or activities that bring joy and relaxation. Self-care can also involve setting boundaries, saying no to things that drain our energy, and seeking help when needed.

Forgive Yourself and Others.

Dealing with past demons often involves forgiving ourselves and others for the pain, hurt, or mistakes of the past. Forgiveness does not mean forgetting or condoning what happened, but it means letting go of the anger, resentment, or bitterness that may be holding us back. Forgiveness can be a difficult and ongoing process, but it can bring a sense of peace, compassion, and freedom.

Take Action.

Dealing with past demons can be overwhelming, but it is important to take action towards healing and growth. This can involve setting goals, making plans, and taking small steps towards positive change. It can also involve facing our fears, challenging negative beliefs, and reframing our perspectives about ourselves and the past. Taking action can bring a sense of empowerment, resilience, and hope.

Practice Gratitude.

Dealing with past demons can sometimes make us feel stuck in negative emotions and memories, but practicing gratitude can help shift our focus towards the positive aspects of our lives. This can involve acknowledging the people, things, and experiences that bring joy, meaning, and purpose to our lives. It can also involve finding gratitude in the challenges and lessons of the past, which can help us grow and evolve as individuals.

In conclusion, dealing with past demons is not easy, but it is possible with the right strategies and support. Acknowledging and accepting the past, seeking professional help, connecting with others, practicing self-care, forgiving ourselves and others, taking action, and practicing gratitude are all important steps towards healing and growth. It is important to remember that everyone's journey towards healing is unique and that there is no right or wrong way to deal with past demons. However, with patience, resilience, and support, it is possible to overcome

I had been taking various medications, including Xanax, Klonopin, Adderall, Abilify, Ritaline, Zoloft, etc., all my life. As a child, it was used to keep me "in line," but as I got older and into my teens, I started to stop taking my medications. When I finished high school, I realized the purpose of all those pills: control. I wouldn't be able to feel or get upset because of it. When Viky did or said something to me, I did not question her. Although I was regarded as a "happy" child, I was actually a controlled and manipulated child who had never experienced childhood. Medication was the solution because I was already very young and was expected to be an adult.

I was off medications by the time I got to college, but when my mother was killed, I went to get help right away because it was too much to handle on my own. I continued taking my medication for a very long time up until 2016, when I found out that all of my partying and taking so many medications as a child had destroyed 20% of my liver. After that, I didn't take any more medications for another four years. Finally, I got the results of a liver test, which showed that my liver was on its way to 100% full recovery. After receiving permission from my doctor, I went back into a psychiatrist's office right away. I decided that I would stop drinking alcohol for as long as I could stand it because I had done so much damage to my liver.

Although I did occasionally fall off, I am now five years sober, and I am extremely proud of that accomplishment.

It's so different to live without alcohol. I no longer frequently experience the shakes, pounding headache, nausea, vomiting, or dizziness. I could get out of bed in the morning without frantically searching the liquor cabinet for my favorite bourbon or tequila. I no longer had to be a slave to the "drink." I wouldn't have to sneak alcohol from coworkers who worked the bar or rush home to drink the alcohol that was waiting for me in my car if I went to work sober. I regret putting myself and other people in danger because I was so desperate for alcohol. Both I and those around me were aware that I was in danger. Even though I was so desperate at the time, when I look back now, I even don't recognize anyone. That is not who I am, and I have gained knowledge from those experiences and have avoided falling back into that hole again.

After watching the world around me be so loud and distracting I've realized that the world will always be loud. No matter what I do or where I go, I will never escape the noise. I've even lived in the woods and still the woods are loud in their own kind of way. It's hard to want silence when there isn't a possibility for it and I have come to accept that reality. We as people are chaotic beings and with that being said there is no way to understand "peace" from a chaotic mind.

The world is constantly in motion and filled with noise. From the hum of cars on the streets to the chatter of people in public spaces, there is always something making a sound. Even in the quiet of the countryside, there are birds singing, leaves rustling, and wind blowing. The noise never truly stops.

As technology advances and the population grows, the amount of noise in the world is likely to increase. Cities will become louder and more densely populated, and industrialization will lead to more machinery and construction. Even in rural areas, the use of technology such as drones and power tools will add to the noise levels.

However, as the noise of the world increases, our ability to block it out or adapt to it will also improve. The use of noise-canceling technology in headphones and earplugs will help us to block out unwanted sounds. In addition, cities and buildings will be designed with sound-proofing materials to create quieter spaces.

Ultimately, the world will never be truly quiet, but our ability to adapt to and control the noise will make it softer in our ears. We will learn to filter out unwanted sounds and focus on the sounds that are important to us. The noise of the world will always be present, but it will no longer be overwhelming or disruptive to our daily lives. Ultimately how the world will never be quiet but only get softer in your ears.

So far, I've achieved to control my anger and replace it with kindness when that wasn't a reality for me. I can look at a situation and analyze it before reacting when I'd react before knowing all the details. I've also grown as a person; I am not so quick to judge anyone and their choices anymore. I listen and try to understand where they are coming from and what they are trying to accomplish in life because you never know what someone has gone through or will go through in their life and kindness is fleeting as it is.

Finally, I conclude this chapter with a letter to myself:

Dear sweet little girl,

I am so sorry that you had to go through all of this. I know your heart and mind are breaking to pieces at this very moment. The world and people around you are not being supportive and you are drowning in your tears. Those people will tell you that they love you and that they care about you but don't believe them. THAT IS NOT LOVE. Once you are able to leave that place, just know, things get WAY BETTER. I know you wanted to end it and tried without success, but the choices you were making were not based on just you, and I am still so very sorry that we will hold this inside forever.

You may not be completely happy but there will be times of happiness that you will create on your own. You will help a few restaurants and run one as a General Manager one day, and you will also learn French cooking techniques from a wild and crazy Cuban Chef who has an obsession with Chef Gordon Ramsey. He will help you go places and give you an opportunity that no one else will be able to provide for you. He will help keep you and your husband afloat and gift you with many things/gifts. Most of all, he will help guide your husband through his passion while you start finding yours. I know, I know, "we don't have goals" but eventually we come around, hahaha.

Sweetheart, I know you were broken, beaten, and told many horrible things, but YOU WILL RISE UP! You will rise up screaming your own name from the rooftops, saying, "YES! I CAN DO THIS! I CAN LIVE A LIFE!" You will wake up every day not hating yourself or life. You will become a person you never thought you could be or know you were this person at all. All the strength you put up into your heart and soul will pay off, I promise. All of this is just a test of time. Time doesn't make things better or heal any wounds. Time makes you realize that that's all we have left in living so when the time comes you will be living a life you couldn't have imagined you could live. You'll own a house, and two cars, have a HUGE backyard, own a cat AND a dog at the same time, and also have a loving husband. Sweetheart, these things will open you up to new feelings, and life experiences. I know life is hard right now and you can't see past all the bad and the sadness, but I am you and will always be with you. I will hold your hand and your head up and high through our struggles. I will stand underneath you to keep you on the right path, for we only have ourselves to rely on sometimes. Sweetheart, just remember:

YOU WILL RISE!

Love you always sweetheart.

Chapter 10: Love Should Never Hurt

"This chapter is for my readers and how they can avoid the red flags in abusive relationships"

Domestic violence is a pervasive issue that affects millions of people worldwide. It is not just physical violence but also emotional, psychological, and financial abuse. Perpetrators of domestic violence use tactics such as gaslighting, manipulation, and control to maintain power and dominance over their partners.

It's important to remember that there is no right or wrong way to grieve. Everyone experiences loss differently, and it's important to allow yourself to feel whatever emotions arise. Some days may be more difficult than others, and that's okay. It's important to be patient and kind to yourself as you navigate this process.

As time passes, you may find that the intensity of your emotions begins to subside. However, it's important to remember that grief is not a linear process and that there may be moments when it resurfaces. This is normal and expected, and it's important to continue to practice self-care and seek support when needed.

MEMORY

The day was warm with a slight chill in the air as the sun was setting, I was sitting in the passenger seat of an ex-boyfriend's F250 long-bed white truck. We were talking about the "what if's" in life and some-how the conversation of us breaking up came into topic. "You know you'd never leave me," he said with a grin on his face. "Oh, really? What makes you think that," I answer back sharply. He then pats the center console and says, "Because my buddy here in the center console, and I, just love you too much and we wouldn't want to see you go". I shivered a little when I heard this and said no more. We road quietly back to his house, in the middle of nowhere, and then he revealed to me who he was referring to as his buddy in the console; his gun. He wasn't very kind to me and didn't say nice things often so this behavior wasn't that much of a surprise. But, I had enough of him acting that way. I grabbed his hand with the gun and put it to my head then pulled the trigger. I closed my eyes waiting for the bang but all I heard was a "CLICK". I opened them and to my amazement he was sitting there with an expression of shock and confusion. I almost ended my own life in front of him, but the gun wasn't even loaded. I had no idea. I called his bluff and made a choice that could have ended my life. To be honest, I was ready to end my life because of the extreme stress I was suddenly under. "You called my bluff," he said in a flat voice. "I'm tired of everyone's shit" I say as I hop out of his truck and start walking through the brush to get the mile and a half to my home. He found me half way through my walk in the wilderness. I had little thorns and cactus needles in my pant legs and shoe laces. He stopped in front of me and said, "Let me give you a ride. If you get home on foot then there will be questions asked. You know I was joking right?" I agreed with him and didn't want to hear it when I got home about why I was walking through the brush, so he gave me a ride home so no one would know what happened. He begged me not to tell anyone and kept insisting it was a joke, but when I got home to my paternal grandparent's home, they knew something was wrong and I told Lupe what happened. He told me to never see him again so I didn't. I also revealed the comments he was making about my weight and the way that I dressed to Lupe and he helped me realize that a man has no say in what a woman wears because it is her body.

A lot of his comments still resonate inside my head when I want to get dressed up for an outing or date-night with my husband. I worry that I am over/underdressed or the clothes are ill-fitting. The psychological games he played with my mind had long-lasting effects.

Abusive relationships can be incredibly damaging, both physically and emotionally. Unfortunately, many people find themselves in these types of relationships, often unaware of the warning signs until it is too late. In this chapter, we will discuss some of the red flags to look out for in abusive relationships and what you can do to avoid them.

Isolation

Isolation is a common tactic used by abusers in relationships to maintain control over their victims. It involves cutting off the victim from their support system, including family, friends, and other forms of social connection. Isolation can take many forms, from preventing the victim from leaving the house to discouraging or forbidding them from talking to other people. Over time, isolation can make the victim feel trapped, alone, and dependent on their abuser, making it more difficult for them to leave the relationship.

Isolation often begins subtly, with the abuser suggesting that they spend more time together or that the victim doesn't need anyone else in their life. The abuser may also criticize the victim's friends or family, saying that they're a bad influence or that they don't really care about the victim. This can make the victim doubt their own relationships and feel like they have to choose between their abuser and the people they care about.

As isolation progresses, the abuser may become more controlling, monitoring the victim's communication with others and limiting their access to the outside world. They may also use threats or physical force to prevent the victim from leaving the house or contacting other people. The abuser may make the victim feel like they're responsible for their own isolation, saying that they're too difficult to be around or that other people don't understand them.

Isolation can have serious psychological effects on the victim. They may feel like they're losing their sense of self and their connection to the outside world. They may become depressed, anxious, or paranoid, feeling like they're being watched or controlled. They may also start to believe that their abuser's version of reality is the only one that matters, losing their ability to make decisions and think for themselves.

Isolation can also make it more difficult for the victim to leave the relationship. They may feel like they have nowhere else to go or no one else to turn to. They may also feel like they're betraying their abuser by leaving, especially if the abuser has convinced them that they're the only person who truly cares about them. This can make it difficult for the victim to reach out for help or even recognize that they're in an abusive situation.

Breaking free from isolation can be a critical step in leaving an abusive relationship. Victims may need to rebuild their support system, reaching out to friends and family or finding new sources of connection. They may also need to seek professional help, such as counseling or therapy, to work through the psychological effects of isolation and abuse. Building a strong support system can help victims feel less alone and more empowered to make decisions about their own lives.

One of the first red flags to look out for in an abusive relationship is isolation. Abusers often try to cut off their victims from their friends and family members, leaving them feeling alone and vulnerable. This can make it much harder for the victim to leave the relationship, as they feel like they have nobody to turn to.

If your partner is trying to isolate you, it is important to reach out to friends and family members for support. You can also seek out support groups or counseling services to help you cope with the abuse.

Controlling Behavior

Controlling behavior is one of the most common forms of abuse in intimate relationships. It involves the use of various tactics by one partner to control and dominate the other partner. The behavior can range from subtle manipulation to outright physical abuse. The effects of controlling behavior can be devastating to the victim, leading to low self-esteem, anxiety, depression, and even physical harm. In this essay, we will explore the various aspects of controlling behavior in an abusive relationship.

One of the main characteristics of controlling behavior is the use of power and control. The abuser uses a variety of tactics to maintain power and control over the victim. These tactics may include physical abuse, emotional abuse, psychological abuse, financial abuse, and sexual abuse. For example, an abuser may prevent the victim from leaving the house, controlling what they wear or eat, monitoring their phone calls or messages, or isolating them from family and friends. These actions serve to isolate the victim from sources of support and increase their dependence on the abuser.

Another aspect of controlling behavior is the use of fear and intimidation. Abusers often use fear and intimidation to keep their victims under control. This may include making threats of physical harm, using physical violence, or manipulating the victim's emotions to make them feel guilty or ashamed. The abuser may use gaslighting techniques to make the victim doubt their own memory, perception, or sanity. They may also engage in verbal abuse or name-calling, which can lead to the victim feeling worthless and powerless.

Controlling behavior is also characterized by the abuser's need for control over every aspect of the victim's life. This includes controlling the victim's access to resources such as money, transportation, and communication. The abuser may demand to know the victim's every move or require them to report their whereabouts at all times. The abuser may also control the victim's access to healthcare, education, or employment. By controlling these areas of the victim's life, the abuser maintains a sense of power and control over the victim.

One of the most insidious aspects of controlling behavior is that it can be difficult to recognize. Many victims of controlling behavior may not even realize that they are being abused. They may believe that the abuser's behavior is normal or that they are to blame for the abuse. Victims may also feel trapped in the relationship and unable to leave due to financial or emotional dependence on the abuser. This can make it difficult for them to seek help or support from friends, family, or professionals.

Controlling behavior can have serious consequences for the victim's mental and physical health. Victims may experience symptoms of anxiety, depression, or post-traumatic stress disorder (PTSD). They may also develop physical symptoms such as headaches, gastrointestinal problems, or chronic pain. The stress and trauma of the abuse can also have long-term effects on the victim's overall health and well-being.

One of the key ways to address controlling behavior in an abusive relationship is to recognize the signs of abuse and seek help. This may include seeking support from friends or family, contacting the National Domestic Violence Hotline at 800-799-7233, or seeking therapy or counseling. Victims may also benefit from legal assistance to obtain protective orders or file criminal charges against the abuser.

Another important step in addressing controlling behavior is to hold the abuser accountable for their actions. This may involve legal consequences such as arrest, prosecution, or imprisonment. It may also involve education and counseling for the abuser to address their controlling behavior and learn healthy relationship skills.

Another common red flag in abusive relationships is controlling behavior. Abusers often try to control every aspect of their partner's life, from what they wear to who they talk to. This can leave the victim feeling powerless and trapped.

If your partner is exhibiting controlling behavior, it is important to set boundaries and assert your independence. You can also seek out counseling services to help you build your self-esteem and confidence.

Verbal Abuse

Verbal abuse is a common form of emotional abuse that can occur in abusive relationships. It involves the use of words and language to control, manipulate, degrade, or intimidate another person. Verbal abuse is often used by an abuser to establish power and control over their partner, and it can be just as damaging as physical abuse.

Verbal abuse can take many forms, and it can be difficult to recognize because it often occurs behind closed doors. Some examples of verbal abuse include name-calling, yelling, screaming, belittling, mocking, gaslighting, and constant criticism. The abuser may also use threats, intimidation, and coercion to control their partner, and may use guilt, shame, or blame to manipulate them.

One of the most damaging aspects of verbal abuse is that it can erode a victim's self-esteem and self-worth. Over time, the victim may begin to believe the negative messages that their abuser is communicating, and may start to doubt their own abilities, worth, and sanity. The victim may also become isolated from their friends and family, as the abuser may try to control their relationships and limit their contact with others.

Verbal abuse can also have physical and psychological effects on the victim. The constant stress and anxiety caused by verbal abuse can lead to physical health problems such as headaches, stomach problems, and insomnia. It can also lead to mental health issues such as depression, anxiety, and post-traumatic stress disorder (PTSD).

In many cases, verbal abuse is a precursor to physical

abuse. The abuser may use verbal abuse as a way to test the victim's boundaries and see how much control they can exert over them. If the victim does not resist or fight back, the abuser may escalate to physical violence.

If you are in an abusive relationship, it is important to recognize the signs of verbal abuse and take steps to protect yourself. Here are some tips for dealing with verbal abuse:

Recognize the signs of verbal abuse: Verbal abuse can take many forms, including name-calling, belittling, yelling, and gaslighting. If you are experiencing any of these behaviors, it is important to recognize them as abuse.

- **Set boundaries**: It is important to set clear boundaries with your abuser and let them know what behavior is unacceptable. You may need to repeat these boundaries multiple times, as abusers often test their victims' boundaries.

- **Seek support**: It is important to seek support from friends, family, or a professional counselor. Talking to someone you trust can help you process your feelings and develop a plan for leaving the abusive relationship.

- **Build your self-esteem**: Verbal abuse can erode your self-esteem and self-worth. It is important to build yourself up by engaging in activities that make you feel good about yourself.

- **Plan for your safety**: If you are in an abusive relationship, it is important to plan for your safety. This may include creating a safety plan, contacting the National Domestic Violence Hotline (800-799-7233), or seeking a protective order.
- **Leave the relationship**: Ultimately, the best way to protect yourself from verbal abuse is to leave the abusive relationship. This may be a difficult decision, but it is important to prioritize your safety and well-being.

In conclusion, verbal abuse is a serious issue that can have long-lasting effects on the victim. It is important to recognize the signs of verbal abuse, set clear boundaries, seek support, build your self-esteem, plan for your safety, and consider leaving the abusive relationship. Remember, you deserve to be treated with respect and dignity, and there is help available if you need it.

If your partner is verbally abusive, it is important to speak up and set boundaries. Let your partner know that their behavior is not acceptable and that you will not tolerate it.

You can also seek out counseling services to help you cope with the abuse.

Physical Abuse

Physical abuse is perhaps the most well-known form of abuse in relationships. This can include hitting, kicking, and other forms of physical violence. Physical abuse can leave the victim with physical injuries as well as emotional scars.

If your partner is physically abusive, it is important to get help immediately. Contact the police or the National Domestic Violence Hotline (800-799-7233) for assistance. You can also seek out counseling services to help you cope with the trauma of the abuse.

Abusive relationships can take many forms, and physical violence is one of the most severe and dangerous. Physical abuse can have a profound impact on a victim's physical and mental health, and it can also be a precursor to more severe violence or even homicide. We will explore some of the physical threats that are commonly associated with abusive relationships.

One of the most common forms of physical abuse in

abusive relationships is hitting or punching. This can result in bruises, cuts, broken bones, and other injuries. Victims of physical abuse may also experience emotional trauma as a result of the violence they have experienced. This trauma can manifest as anxiety, depression, or post-traumatic stress disorder (PTSD), and it can have long-lasting effects on a person's mental health.

Another physical threat that is commonly associated with abusive relationships is choking or strangulation. This type of violence can be particularly dangerous because it can lead to brain damage or death within minutes. In fact, strangulation is one of the leading causes of domestic violence-related deaths. Victims of this type of abuse may experience shortness of breath, dizziness, and loss of consciousness. If left untreated, these symptoms can become life-threatening.

Sexual abuse is another physical threat that is commonly associated with abusive relationships. This can include unwanted touching, rape, and other forms of sexual assault. Victims of sexual abuse may experience physical injuries, such as bruises or lacerations, as well as emotional trauma, such as feelings of shame, guilt, or fear. Sexual abuse can also result in the transmission of sexually transmitted infections (STIs) or unwanted pregnancy.

In addition to these specific forms of physical abuse, abusive relationships can also involve more general threats to a victim's physical safety. This can include verbal threats of violence, destruction of property, or stalking. These types of behaviors can create a pervasive sense of fear and anxiety in a victim, and they can also make it difficult for the victim to leave the abusive relationship.

There are several risk factors that may increase a person's likelihood of experiencing physical abuse in an abusive relationship. These can include a history of violence or abuse in the family, a lack of social support, low self-esteem, and financial dependence on the abuser. Victims may also be more vulnerable to physical abuse during periods of stress, such as during a pandemic, when economic instability is high, or when they are going through a difficult life transition.

If you or someone you know is experiencing physical abuse in an abusive relationship, it is important to seek help as soon as possible. There are several resources available for victims of domestic violence, including hotlines, shelters, and counseling services. In some cases, it may be necessary to involve law enforcement or to obtain a restraining order to ensure the victim's safety.

In conclusion, physical threats are a significant concern in abusive relationships. Victims of physical abuse may experience a range of physical and emotional injuries, and they may be at risk for more severe violence or even homicide. It is important to take physical threats seriously and to seek help as soon as possible if you or someone you know is experiencing abuse in a relationship. With the right support and resources, victims can find safety and healing, and they can move towards a brighter future free from violence and abuse.

Gaslighting

Gaslighting is a form of emotional abuse in which the abuser manipulates their partner into questioning their own reality. This can leave the victim feeling confused and unsure of themselves.

Gaslighting is a form of manipulation that tries to make factual information look like hazy confusion. It is a vehement assertion that what happened didn't really happen or was different from what actually happened. You might think you're going mad when gaslighting occurs. You doubt not only the facts but also your memory. Gaslighting can make you feel depressed and lost, making you doubt your own decision-making abilities. It is designed to accomplish exactly that. It is one of the most potent indicators of emotional abuse. It is a flagrant attempt to shape the truth to the gas lighter's advantage, not only over you and your thoughts but also over the narrative.

If your partner is gaslighting you, it is important to speak up and assert your reality. Let your partner know that their behavior is not acceptable and that you will not tolerate it. You can also seek out counseling services to help you build your self-esteem and confidence.

Gaslighting is a form of psychological manipulation that aims to make a person doubt their own perceptions, memories, and sanity. It is a subtle and insidious form of emotional abuse that can be difficult to recognize, as it often involves gradual and subtle forms of manipulation that can gradually wear down a person's self-esteem and self-confidence. We will examine the nature of gaslighting, how it works, and the effects it can have on the victim.

The term "gaslighting" originates from the 1944 movie "Gaslight," in which a man manipulates his wife into doubting her own sanity by secretly dimming the gaslights in their home and then denying that anything is amiss. Gaslighting can take many forms, however, and does not always involve such overt and theatrical manipulations. In fact, it often takes the form of more subtle and insidious forms of emotional abuse, such as minimizing a person's feelings, denying their experiences, and dismissing their concerns.

One of the key ways in which gaslighting works is through the use of lies and deception. A gaslighter will often lie about things that are easily verifiable, such as events that have occurred or conversations that have taken place. By doing so, they can make the victim doubt their own memories and perceptions, and begin to question their own sanity. Additionally, gas lighters will often deny that certain things have happened or that certain conversations have taken place, which can further undermine the victim's sense of reality.

Another common tactic used by gaslighters is to question the victim's perception of events or their own feelings. They may tell the victim that they are being too sensitive or overreacting, or they may suggest that the victim is misinterpreting what is happening. This can lead the victim to doubt their own feelings and emotions, and can make them feel as though they are not entitled to their own thoughts and feelings.

Gaslighting can also take the form of projection, in

which the gaslighter accuses the victim of things that they themselves are guilty of. For example, a gaslighter may accuse their partner of being unfaithful, when in fact it is the gaslighter who is cheating. This can further undermine the victim's sense of reality and can make them doubt their own perceptions of what is happening.

The effects of gaslighting can be devastating for the victim. They may begin to doubt their own sanity, and may feel as though they are losing touch with reality. They may feel isolated and alone, as they may find it difficult to trust anyone or to confide in others. They may also experience a range of emotional and physical symptoms, including anxiety, depression, insomnia, and physical ailments such as headaches and stomach problems.

Gaslighting can be particularly damaging in relationships, as it can make the victim feel trapped and powerless. They may feel as though they are unable to leave the relationship, as they have been convinced that they are the problem and that they are responsible for the gaslighter's behavior. This can make it difficult for them to seek help or to speak out about what is happening, as they may feel as though they are to blame.

If you suspect that you are being gaslighted, there are

a number of things you can do to protect yourself. First and foremost, it is important to trust your own perceptions and feelings. If something feels off or doesn't seem right, it probably isn't. It can also be helpful to keep a record of what is happening, including any conversations or interactions that take place. This can help to provide evidence of what is happening, and can be helpful if you decide to seek help or support.

Jealousy

Jealousy is another red flag to look out for in abusive relationships. Abusers often become jealous when their partner interacts with other people, even in non-romantic ways. This can lead to controlling behavior and isolation.

If your partner is exhibiting jealousy, it is important to set boundaries and assert your independence. Let your partner know that their behavior is not acceptable and that you will not tolerate it. You can also seek out counseling services to help you cope with the abuse.

Jealousy is a complex emotion that arises when we perceive a threat to something we value, such as a relationship or possession. It is a common human emotion, experienced by people of all ages, cultures, and genders. While jealousy is a natural emotion, it can become problematic when it takes over our lives and affects our relationships and mental health. We will explore the different aspects of jealousy, its causes, effects, and ways to deal with it.

Jealousy is a feeling of envy or resentment towards someone else's success, advantages, or possessions. It is an emotion that arises when we feel threatened by someone who has something that we do not. For instance, a person may feel jealous when their partner spends time with someone else, or when their colleague gets a promotion. Jealousy is often accompanied by a range of physical and emotional reactions, such as anxiety, fear, anger, and sadness.

There are different types of jealousy, including romantic jealousy, sibling jealousy, and envy towards friends or acquaintances. Romantic jealousy is perhaps the most common type, and it arises when a person feels threatened by their partner's attention or affection towards someone else. Sibling jealousy, on the other hand, is common among children and arises when a child feels that their parents favor one sibling over the other. Jealousy towards friends or acquaintances may arise when a person feels envious of someone else's success or happiness.

The causes of jealousy are complex and varied. One of the main causes is insecurity. When a person feels insecure about themselves or their relationship, they are more likely to experience jealousy. For instance, a person who lacks self-confidence may feel jealous when their partner spends time with someone who is more outgoing or attractive. Another cause of jealousy is past experiences. If a person has been betrayed or hurt in the past, they may be more sensitive to potential threats and therefore experience jealousy more often.

Jealousy can have both positive and negative effects. In some cases, jealousy can motivate a person to work harder or to improve themselves. For instance, a person who feels jealous of their colleague's promotion may work harder to achieve similar success. However, jealousy can also have negative effects on a person's mental health and relationships. Jealousy can lead to feelings of anxiety, depression, and anger, which can affect a person's overall well-being. Jealousy can also damage relationships by causing trust issues, conflicts, and resentment.

Dealing with jealousy can be challenging, but there are several strategies that can help. One of the most effective strategies is to identify the root cause of the jealousy. By understanding why you feel jealous, you can address the underlying issue and work towards resolving it. For instance, if you feel jealous of your partner's attention towards someone else, you may need to work on your own self-esteem and trust issues.

Another strategy is to communicate openly and honestly with your partner or loved ones. By expressing your feelings and concerns, you can build trust and understanding, which can help to reduce jealousy. It is important to communicate in a non-confrontational way and to listen to the other person's perspective.

Learning to manage your emotions can also help to reduce jealousy. This may involve practicing mindfulness, meditation, or other relaxation techniques to help you stay calm and centered. It may also involve learning to reframe your thoughts and beliefs about jealousy. For instance, instead of seeing jealousy as a sign of weakness, you can view it as a natural emotion that can be managed and controlled.

Finally, seeking professional help may be necessary in some cases. If jealousy is affecting your mental health or relationships, it may be helpful to seek therapy or counseling. A trained therapist can help you identify the root causes of your jealousy and develop strategies to manage it effectively

Threats

Abusive relationships can be incredibly harmful and can have a profound impact on the physical and emotional well-being of the victim. One of the most significant risks associated with an abusive relationship is the threat of violence. This threat can manifest in a variety of ways, including physical, emotional, and psychological abuse. We will explore the various types of threat in abusive relationships and the impact they can have on the victim.

Abusive relationships are one of the most dangerous and prevalent issues in our society. They occur when one partner uses physical, emotional, or psychological tactics to control and manipulate the other. In many cases, the victim is too scared or too ashamed to leave the relationship, leaving them trapped in a cycle of abuse. This can lead to serious consequences, including physical injury, emotional trauma, and even death.

Threats are a common tactic used by abusers to maintain power and control over their victims. These threats can take many forms, including threats of physical violence, emotional manipulation, financial control, and isolation from family and friends. They can be explicit or implicit, overt or subtle, and can be made in person, over the phone, through text messages, or via social media.

Physical threats are perhaps the most obvious type of threat in an abusive relationship. Abusers may threaten to hit, punch, kick, or even kill their victims if they do not comply with their demands. These threats can be extremely frightening, especially if the abuser has a history of violence. Victims may feel trapped and unable to escape, especially if they have children or other dependents to protect.

Emotional threats are also common in abusive relationships. Abusers may use emotional manipulation to control their victims, such as by threatening to leave them, to harm themselves, or to harm others. They may also use gaslighting, a tactic in which they manipulate their victims into doubting their own perceptions and memories, making it harder for them to trust their own judgment.

Financial control is another tactic used by abusers to maintain power over their victims. They may threaten to withhold money, to prevent their victims from working, or to ruin their credit if they do not comply with their demands. This can leave victims feeling trapped and dependent on their abusers, making it harder for them to leave the relationship.

Isolation is also a common tactic used by abusers to control their victims. They may threaten to harm or even kill their victims' family members or friends if they try to leave the relationship. They may also prevent their victims from seeing their loved ones, making it harder for them to get help or support.

One of the most insidious aspects of threats in abusive relationships is that they can escalate over time. What may start as a seemingly harmless threat can quickly spiral out of control, leading to more serious forms of abuse. This is why it is so important for victims to seek help as soon as possible, before the situation becomes even more dangerous.

If you or someone you know is in an abusive relationship, it is important to seek help immediately. There are many resources available for victims of abuse, including hotlines, shelters, and support groups. You can also speak to a therapist or counselor who can help you develop a safety plan and provide emotional support.

It is important to remember that abuse is never the victim's fault. Abusers are solely responsible for their actions, and victims should not feel ashamed or guilty for being in an abusive relationship. The most important thing is to take steps to protect yourself and get the help you need to break free from the cycle of abuse.

In conclusion, threats are a common and dangerous tactic used by abusers to maintain power and control over their victims. These threats can take many forms, including physical violence, emotional manipulation, financial control, and isolation. It is important for victims to seek help as soon as possible, before the situation escalates and becomes even more dangerous. Remember, abuse is never the victim's fault, and there are resources available to help you break free from an abusive relationship.

Physical Threats

Physical threats are one of the most visible and obvious forms of threat in abusive relationships. Physical abuse can include hitting, slapping, punching, and kicking, among other things. These actions are intended to inflict physical harm on the victim and can leave lasting injuries. Victims of physical abuse may suffer from broken bones, bruises, and cuts, as well as long-term health problems like chronic pain and neurological damage.

The threat of physical violence can be just as

damaging as the act itself. Abusers may use physical intimidation to control their partners, making them feel powerless and helpless. This can lead to a sense of constant fear and anxiety, as victims never know when their abuser may strike next. This fear can also make it difficult for victims to leave the relationship, as they may feel that leaving would put them at even greater risk of harm.

Emotional Threats

Emotional abuse is another common form of threat in abusive relationships. Emotional abuse can include name-calling, belittling, and humiliating behavior. Abusers may also use emotional manipulation to control their partners, using guilt or shame to keep them in line. This type of abuse can be particularly insidious, as it is often difficult to recognize and can leave lasting emotional scars.

Emotional threats are a form of psychological abuse that can occur in abusive relationships. Emotional threats can take many different forms, from subtle manipulation to overt threats of violence. They are often used by abusers as a way to control their partners and maintain power and dominance over them. In this essay, we will explore the different types of emotional threats that can occur in abusive relationships and the impact they can have on victims.

One of the most common forms of emotional threat is verbal abuse. This can include name-calling, belittling, and other forms of verbal aggression. Verbal abuse can be especially damaging because it can wear down a victim's self-esteem and confidence over time. Victims may begin to believe the negative things their abusers say about them, which can lead to feelings of worthlessness and self-doubt.

Another form of emotional threat is isolation. Abusers may try to control their partners by limiting their access to friends and family members. This can be done by preventing them from leaving the house, monitoring their phone and internet use, and other means. Isolation can be particularly dangerous because it can make it difficult for victims to seek help or escape from abusive situations.

Threats of physical violence are another common form of emotional threat in abusive relationships. Abusers may threaten to harm their partners if they do not comply with their demands or if they try to leave. These threats can be incredibly frightening and can make victims feel as though they are constantly in danger. Even if the abuser does not act on these threats, the fear and anxiety they cause can be incredibly damaging to victims' mental health.

Financial abuse is another form of emotional threat

that can occur in abusive relationships. Abusers may try to control their partners by limiting their access to money or by using money as a means of control. This can include refusing to allow their partners to work, controlling all financial decisions, and other means. Financial abuse can make it difficult for victims to leave abusive situations because they may feel as though they have no means of supporting themselves.

Gaslighting is another form of emotional threat that can occur in abusive relationships. Gaslighting involves the abuser manipulating their partner's perception of reality. This can include denying things that have happened, making the victim doubt their memory, and other means. Gaslighting can be particularly insidious because it can make victims feel as though they are losing their minds. It can also make it difficult for victims to trust their own perceptions and judgment.

Emotional threats can have a profound impact on victims of abuse. They can lead to feelings of fear, anxiety, and depression. Victims may become isolated and withdrawn, which can make it difficult for them to seek help or support. Emotional threats can also have long-lasting effects on victims' mental health, even after they have left abusive relationships.

It is important for anyone who is experiencing emotional threats in a relationship to seek help and support. This can include reaching out to friends and family members, contacting the National Domestic Violence Hotline (800-799-7233), or seeking counseling. It is also important for society as a whole to recognize the impact of emotional threats in abusive relationships and to work to create a culture in which abuse of any kind is not tolerated.

In conclusion, emotional threats are a form of psychological abuse that can occur in abusive relationships. They can take many different forms, from verbal abuse to isolation to threats of physical violence. Emotional threats can have a profound impact on victims' mental health and well-being, and it is important for anyone experiencing them to seek help and support. It is also important for society as a whole to work to create a culture in which abuse of any kind is not tolerated.

The threat of emotional abuse can be just as damaging as the abuse itself. Victims may feel trapped in the relationship, as their abuser has convinced them that they are worthless and unlovable. This can lead to a sense of isolation and hopelessness, as victims may believe that they have no one to turn to for help. The emotional toll of abuse can be just as devastating as physical abuse, leading to long-term mental health problems like depression and anxiety.

Psychological Threats

Psychological abuse is another common form of threat in abusive relationships. This type of abuse can include gaslighting, where the abuser tries to convince the victim that they are crazy or delusional. Abusers may also threaten to harm themselves or others if their partner leaves them, using fear to control their behavior. This type of abuse can be particularly difficult to recognize, as it often takes the form of subtle manipulation.

Psychological threats are a common feature of abusive relationships. These threats can take many forms, including verbal abuse, emotional manipulation, and intimidation. Psychological threats can be incredibly damaging, and they can have long-lasting effects on a person's mental and emotional well-being.

One of the most common forms of psychological threat in abusive relationships is verbal abuse. This can take many different forms, including yelling, screaming, belittling, and name-calling. Verbal abuse can be incredibly damaging, and it can make a person feel worthless and powerless. It can also make it difficult for a person to trust themselves or their own judgment.

Another common form of psychological threat in abusive relationships is emotional manipulation. Emotional manipulation can take many different forms, but it generally involves one person using emotional tactics to control or manipulate the other person. This can include things like guilt-tripping, gaslighting, and playing mind games. Emotional manipulation can be incredibly damaging, and it can make it difficult for a person to trust their own emotions and instincts.

Intimidation is another common form of psychological threat in abusive relationships. Intimidation can take many different forms, including physical threats, threats to harm a person's loved ones, and threats to ruin a person's reputation or livelihood. Intimidation can be incredibly frightening, and it can make it difficult for a person to feel safe or secure in their own home.

One of the most insidious forms of psychological threat in abusive relationships is isolation. Isolation involves one person cutting the other person off from their friends, family, and support network. This can make it difficult for a person to leave an abusive relationship, as they may feel like they have no one to turn to. Isolation can also make it difficult for a person to maintain their mental and emotional health, as they may feel lonely and unsupported.

Psychological threats can have many different effects on a person's mental and emotional health. Some of the most common effects of psychological threats in abusive relationships include anxiety, depression, post-traumatic stress disorder (PTSD), and substance abuse. Psychological threats can also make it difficult for a person to trust others, which can lead to problems in future relationships.

If you are experiencing psychological threats in your relationship, it is important to seek help. There are many different resources available to help you leave an abusive relationship and get the support you need to heal. Some of the most common resources for people in abusive relationships include the National Domestic Violence Hotline (800-799-7233), shelters, and support groups.

It is also important to remember that you are not alone. Many people have experienced psychological threats in their relationships, and there is no shame in seeking help. By reaching out for support, you can take the first step towards healing and building a healthier, happier life.

If you are worried that someone you know may be experiencing psychological threats in their relationship, there are several signs to watch out for. These signs may include changes in behavior, such as becoming more withdrawn or anxious, as well as physical signs of abuse, such as bruises or cuts.

If you suspect that someone you know is experiencing psychological threats in their relationship, it is important to offer your support and let them know that you are there for them. You can also offer to help them find resources for leaving an abusive relationship, such as a domestic violence hotline or shelter.

In conclusion, psychological threats are a common feature of abusive relationships. These threats can take many different forms, including verbal abuse, emotional manipulation, intimidation, and isolation. Psychological threats can have long-lasting effects on a person's mental and emotional health, and it is important to seek help if you are experiencing them. By reaching out for support, you can take the first step towards healing and building a healthier, happier life.

The threat of psychological abuse can be just as damaging as the abuse itself. Victims may feel as though they are losing their grip on reality, as their abuser constantly undermines their sense of self-worth and confidence. This can lead to a sense of confusion and self-doubt, as victims struggle to understand what is happening to them. The psychological toll of abuse can be just as devastating as physical abuse, leading to long-term mental health problems like post-traumatic stress disorder (PTSD) and complex trauma.

Impact on the Victim

The impact of threat in abusive relationships can be profound, leaving lasting scars on the victim. Victims may experience a range of physical and emotional symptoms, including anxiety, depression, and insomnia. They may also suffer from physical health problems like chronic pain and digestive issues, as well as long-term mental health problems like PTSD.

The impact of threat in abusive relationships can also extend to the victim's relationships with others. Victims may find it difficult to trust others, as they have been conditioned to believe that they are unworthy of love and respect. This can lead to social isolation and a sense of loneliness, as victims struggle to connect with others.

Threats are another common form of abuse in relationships. Abusers often use threats to control their partner, either by threatening physical harm or by threatening to leave. This can leave the victim feeling powerless and trapped.

If your partner is threatening you, it is important to get help immediately. Contact the police or the National Domestic Violence Hotline (800-799-7233) for assistance. You can also seek out counseling services to help you cope with the trauma of the abuse.

Finally, it's important to remember that your loved one will always be remembered. Even though they may no longer be with us in a physical sense, their memory and the impact they had on your life will continue to live on. Finding ways to honor their memory can be a helpful way to cope with grief and keep their legacy alive.

Losing a loved one too soon is a painful experience that no one should have to go through. However, with time, support, and self-care, it is possible to find healing and peace. Remember that you are not alone in your grief, and that it's okay to reach out for help when you need it.

I had seen the effects of domestic violence firsthand when my mother was killed by her abusive partner. It was a tragedy that left me with a deep sense of grief and loss. I felt as though I had lost a part of myself, and the pain was unbearable at times. My mother had been a kind and loving person, but her partner had taken advantage of her vulnerability and used her love as a weapon against me.

After my mother's death, I was determined to speak out about domestic violence and raise awareness about its devastating effects.

Love should never hurt, and it's important to remember that healthy relationships are built on mutual respect, trust, and care. When love is healthy, it can bring us joy, comfort, and support.

However, it's also important to recognize that sometimes love can be complicated and messy. Relationships can involve conflict and challenges, and it's important to communicate openly and honestly with your partner in order to work through these issues in a healthy way.

It's crucial to remember that any form of abuse, whether it be physical, emotional, or verbal, is never acceptable in a relationship. If you or someone you know is experiencing abuse or violence in a relationship, it's important to seek help and support from professionals and loved ones who can help you stay safe and find a way out of the situation.

Ultimately, it's important to prioritize your own well-being and happiness in any relationship. If you're in a relationship that is causing you pain or making you feel unsafe, it may be time to reassess whether it's truly healthy for you. Remember that you deserve to be loved and treated with respect, and that you have the power to make choices that prioritize your own well-being.

In this chapter I will tell you from experience what you need to do and look out for when it comes to abusive relationships, be if family, friends or spouses.

It is impossible to have an emotionally abusive relationship without assigning blame and guilt. The abuser focuses on the weaknesses in the survivor's response rather than their bad behavior. In order to support their claim that the victim is to blame, the abuser may even pretend to be the victim. The abuser will insist that the victim admit guilt and feel shame as a follow-up to ensure that the victim takes the blame. They reinforce their erroneous belief that they did nothing wrong and that the survivor is solely to blame when they succeed.

Everyone sometimes denies responsibility for wrongdoing, whether it's because they're hurting from shame, can't admit they made a mistake, or something else. It is typical human behavior and rarely targets a single individual. Instead, it's a problem within. When an abuser consistently rejects responsibility for their actions, tries to shift the focus, or explains it away to the survivor in the form of, "I did it for you," it is a red flag that the behavior is turning into emotional abuse. They will use any excuse to avoid taking responsibility and project it externally onto others.

An aggressive attitude is an attempt to control others and the environment and appear larger or more significant than one actually is. It frequently results from a low self-esteem and sense of insecurity. Minor disagreements can give way to hyper aggression, rage, and other sociopathic or psychopathic outbursts. When a person uses emotional abuse to control, manipulate, and hurt a victim, a confrontational attitude is a warning sign. The abuser believes that the victim "deserves it" and that they are the judge and jury.

Isolation is yet another significant relationship red flag. In order to save the survivor, it is intended to cut them off from any backup or support system. Additionally, it keeps the abuser's methods and actions hidden. It is normal for people to be a little jealous, but when that jealousy turns into an obsession or suffocation of the other person, it is an indication of emotional abuse. You must be able to spot it. It can be a big problem when a new relationship moves too quickly, the other person monitors or interferes with communications, causes frequent jealousy fights, or blames you. Any of these could quickly turn into issues with control and could point to the emotional abuser.

Belittling or diminishing talk may appear to be harmless because it is common practice in non-abusive relationships to play games with one another. An emotional red flag of abuse is when it becomes a constant degrading strategy to undermine or control. It is a manipulative strategy to keep control over the abuser and make the victim smaller than the abuser. It comes in the form of ridicule, shaming, criticism, and insults. The abuser will almost always try to cover up by saying things like "it's a joke" or "it's a two-way street."

Frequently, an emotional abuser will have a history of this kind of behavior. It may occasionally be a societal standard that has been passed down through generations. Sometimes, it comes from trauma from the past. All of that doesn't change the fact that abusive behavior in the past is a warning sign that it will continue. As a form of gaslighting, the inability to compromise and emotional invalidation are red flags. By insisting that you are always wrong, overreacting, or lying, the abuser strips you of your ability to defend yourself against them. You are persuaded that you are ignorant, stupid, and have no right to complain.

A lack of trust can often result in unnecessary false accusations and interrogations, which can be a sign of emotional abuse. They are harmful to both the person receiving them and the relationship. An angry personality and behavior indicate that emotional abuse may be occurring in a relationship because it gives the abuser complete manipulative control and takes power away from the victim. Anger can quickly escalate into a potentially fatal physical assault. It can be devastating for the victim's emotional well-being.

So this is it, the last part is a letter from me to you, thank you for taking the time out to know my story.

Letter To Reader

I'm glad we came across each other, and I hope this book helped you along your journey. I am saddened by the fact that this is your wake-up call if you have experienced domestic violence or are just realizing it. Please be assured that a way out will always exist. Simply letting someone know what's going on can significantly improve your "situation." An off-putting joke, a smile, those three little words that make you smile from ear to ear, or even gifts can conceal domestic violence.

When someone loves you, they shouldn't make you think you're the problem; rather, they should take responsibility for their actions. People should never be able to say hurtful things over and over again. You should never respond to verbal abuse that you know is not true about you. Protect yourself. Love who you are. Although it is wonderful to love someone and feel as though they love you back, you must reserve some love for yourself in order to respect yourself and your feelings to the point where you can say, "That was rude of you to say to me" or "That's not true and you know it!" something of that magnitude to reach YOUR END POINT. Make use of the voice you have! We cannot merely accept the circumstances as they are. Even though

181

change is initially scary and difficult, you won't know what you can and cannot do unless you take that leap of faith. When the warning signs start to appear, we need to be brave and take the necessary actions to escape. Keep in mind that only take a chance to show you who they really are only takes one chance.

They will charm you because they have a chance on you back multiple times if you give them chances after chance. Be stern! Be brave! Describe your feelings and the person they're playing with! Don't let someone use your love as a weapon against you! Love is not for the weak! Use your love to spread happiness and light throughout the world, and if anyone wants to harm you or dim your light, they must leave!

Dearest reader, all I can offer is this brief piece of advice, which you can take as you see fit. Just know that you are not alone. Numerous people from all walks of life are affected by domestic violence. There is no one type of domestic violence that is specifically addressed. You can be attacked with weapons made of words, actions, gifts, and even the phrase "I love you." Whenever you can, be aware of your feelings and speak up about them.

Author's Note

Dear Reader,

Thank you, firstly, for giving this a complete chance. I am an average person sharing something that has haunted me for many years and all I can say is Thank You. Thank you for reading my story, thank you for helping keep my mother's memory/story alive because many men and women die from domestic violence because it was too late or no one knew.

I hope my book has touched you and reached out to you in a positive and informative way. All I ask is you take this information and if you see the warning signs of domestic violence/abuse, please say something, video what is happening for evidence, keep all interaction truthful and honest so all parties are held accountable, and be compassionate. You don't know what someone is going through and they may be on the edge waiting for that little helping hand to get them off of that ledge.

I appreciate your time and consideration for my book/story. May you have many blessings and happiness in your life for the rest of your life time. Thank You.

Yours respectfully,

Marissa Pope

Hotline Services

- The National Domestic Violence Hotline: 800-799-7233
  Hours: 24/7
  Languages: English, Spanish and 200 + through interpretation service.
  https://www.thehotline.org/

- National Sexual Assault Hotline: 1-800-656-4673
  Hours: Available 24 hours
  https://www.rainn.org/about-national-sexual-assault-telephone-hotline

- 988 Suicide and Crisis Lifeline: 988
  Hours: Available 24 hours.
  Languages: English, Spanish
  https://988lifeline.org/

- SAMHSA's National Helpline: 1-800-662-4357
  SAMHSA's National Helpline is a free, confidential, 24/7, 365-day-a-year treatment referral and information service (in English and Spanish) for individuals and families facing mental and/or substance use disorders.
  https://www.samhsa.gov/find-help/national-helpline

www.ingramcontent.com/pod-product-compliance
Lightning Source LLC
Chambersburg PA
CBHW051519120626
46551CB00012B/997